WINGBEATS

...kson is a poet, librettist, scriptwriter and director. For thirteen years he was director of Chol Theatre, the pioneering intercultural company based in Huddersfield, and led projects throughout the north of England and in Bangladesh. He has written plays for Oldham Coliseum, Peshkar Productions and an acclaimed trilogy for Burnley Youth Theatre.

Two collections of his poetry have been published, *An Indian Rug Surprised by Snow* (Wrecking Ball, 2005) and *Tear up the lace* (Graft, 2011). He has been Poet in Residence for Ilkley Literature Festival and Schools' Poet in Residence for Bridlington Poetry Festival. In 2010 he won the ...re Prize in the Yorkshire Open Poetry Competition. He lives in West Yorkshire and is currently Teaching Fellow in Creative Writing at the University of Leeds.

THE COMPOSERS

Stephen Kilpatrick is a composer of contemporary instrumental and electronic music. He began his career as a rock and jazz guitarist before going on to study composition with Michael Finnissy and Alan E. Williams. Stephen was born in the UK and studied music at the Universities of Manchester and Salford. From 2001 he spent four years living, studying and working in Hungary, where he developed his interest in Hungarian music.

Cheryl Frances-Hoad is a composer who has been working to commission since she won a prize in the BBC Young Composer Competition at 15. She is currently the Music Fellow with Rambert Dance, and in 2010 she became the youngest composer to win two awards in the same year at the BASCA British Composer Awards. From 2010 to 2012 she was DARE Fellow in Opera Related Arts for Opera North and the University of Leeds.

WINGBEATS

Flight Paths
&
Amy's Last Dive

Written by
Adam Strickson

Composed by
Stephen Kilpatrick
&
Cheryl Frances-Hoad

VALLEY PRESS

First published 2012 by Valley Press
Woodend, The Crescent, Scarborough, YO11 2PW
www.valleypressuk.com

ISBN 978 1 908853 14 1
Cat. no. VP0040

Copyright © Adam Strickson & contributors 2012

The right of Adam Strickson to be identified as the
author of this work has been asserted in accordance with
the Copyright, Designs and Patents Act 1988

All rights reserved. No part of this publication may be
reproduced, stored in or introduced into a retrieval system, or
transmitted in any form, by any means (electronic, mechanical,
photocopying, recording or otherwise) without the prior written
permission of the rights holders.

A CIP catalogue record for this book is
available from the British Library.

Printed and bound in Great Britain by
Imprint Digital, Upton Pyne, Exeter.

This book is sold subject to the condition that it shall not,
by way of trade or otherwise, be lent, re-sold, hired out,
or otherwise circulated without the publisher's prior consent
in any form of binding or cover other than that in which
it is published and without a similar condition, including this
condition, being imposed on the subsequent purchaser.

Wingbeats was part of imove, a Cultural Olympiad programme
in Yorkshire, funded by Legacy Trust UK, creating a lasting impact
from the London 2012 Olympic and Paralympic Games
by funding ideas and local talent to inspire creativity across the UK.

The musical score for *Amy's Last Dive* (ISMN 979 0 57047 187 4)
is published by Cadenza Music (www.cadenza-music.com)

www.valleypressuk.com/books/wingbeats
www.imoveand.com/wingbeats

Contents

Foreword 7

Before the operas

Introduction 11
Beginnings and a plan 14
Poems and songs 19

Flight Paths or *Hope is the thing with feathers*

Birds, women, and writing 37
The writer's compositional plan 44
Extracts from a creative diary 45
Company and cast 52
Characters 56
Libretto 57

Amy's Last Dive

Introduction 95
Extracts from *Amy's Last Dive: Diary of an Opera* 101
Company and cast 126
Characters 130
Libretto 131

Acknowledgements 179
DVD contents 180

Foreword

In the winter of 2009 I was sitting in a dark basement office in central Leeds when an artist posed the question, 'How do we fly without leaving the ground?' to three representatives from imove.

That artist was Adam Strickson and the question eventually resulted in an imove commission and a creative journey that took us from Leeds to the starkly beautiful rural landscape of the East Riding, its associations with the pilot Amy Johnson and aviation, and its internationally significant colonies of seabirds.

Through Wingbeats, Adam, together with a group of talented regional and international artists, created an ambitious programme of work inspired by Flamborough Head and its birds and the Amy Johnson collection at Sewerby Hall in Bridlington. This was work that told stories about the emotional and physical relationship we have with landscape, and harnessed the transformative and transcending power of music and creative movement.

It has been a pleasure to be just a small part of this three-year project, which could not have happened without the support of a huge range of partners, ranging from the RSPB and East Riding of Yorkshire Council to local amateur music organisations. imove was a programme to showcase the very best of our region's arts, culture and heritage to a world audience and Wingbeats certainly delivered.

Jenny Harris
Creative Producer, imove, 2009-2012

BEFORE THE OPERAS

Introduction

TAKE OFF
  SPREAD YOUR WINGS
    SOAR TO NEW HEIGHTS...

I am passionate about the landscape and people of the East Riding and have been working in and around Bridlington for ten years, even though I live at the opposite side of Yorkshire, just over the border from Greater Manchester. So, in 2009, when I saw an opportunity for arts projects for the Olympics connecting with 'Landscape and Heritage' a shining window of opportunity opened. Every year the RSPB reserve at Bempton Cliffs attracts thousands of visitors from all over the region, the country and the world. My ambition was to make theatre in some way equal to the scale and excitement of the towering cliffs, hoping to attract artists and audiences from the region and well beyond.

I'm also passionate about making connections between things and people. I seized the opportunity to bring two different parts of Yorkshire together, Leeds and the East Riding, so that the country could meet the city, and vice versa. Leeds is a large, ambitious city of many cultures that can sometimes seem a long way physically and conceptually from the North Sea frets and the towering cliffs. I wanted to bring the vibrancy and the wildness together through telling life stories of risk, challenge and healing – the kind of healing that can come when we decide to take a deliberate journey or quest through a landscape.

So how did I get to these stories? What was the intuitive insight that started the journey?

One day in early July 2009 I walked from Sewerby Hall to

Flamborough Head. Having visited the evocative Amy Johnson collection, I followed the coast as kittiwakes called and herring gulls screamed. At Flamborough Head, I looked down on hovering kestrels. Flying seemed to be in my head and all around me – I wanted to fly! So I thought, 'How can we fly without leaving the ground?' Over two years, Wingbeats has explored this question. Groups of local school children, university students, amateur and professional singers, musicians, visual artists, dancers and writers have flown in many different and exciting ways, enjoying an amazing 'winged' journey. We've danced on beaches and cliffs, watched a Gypsy Moth loop the loop above us at Sewerby, brought a top string quartet from New York to a small village school and been inspired again and again by the miracle of the seabirds at Bempton. And at the centre of things has been the creation of two new operas made with professionals and community participants, both of which have their origins in that first walk from Sewerby to Flamborough Head.

But why are two 'operas' the centre of the project? For thirty years I've been bringing cultures together by making theatre that has involved a great range of art forms, from shadow puppetry to digital imagery, Kathakali to clog dancing and Persian poetry to rap. By exploring connections between apparently disparate things, and by making work that emerges from the lives of real people, I hope to create new and original work that is equal to the cultural complexity of the times we live in. I have persistently made contemporary stories set in real places with professionals of the highest quality and participants of all ages from that place, believing that the 'raw and the cooked' of this recipe result in an exciting, risky and spicy casserole of theatre which still has the taste of the earth it comes from. I have often made stories about people at the edge of things – refugees, survivors, misfits and outliers – in relation to their experiences of war, famine, poverty, agony, ecstasy, discovery and despair. Away from the high art connotations of the word, opera is simply total theatre that resounds with the extremes of experience, so a journey into its possibilities seemed a logical extension of my journey.

Erin, the heroine of *Flight Paths*, is a single mum from Leeds with a terminally ill mother who works out how to 'fly' her life beyond despair by watching the birds and talking to women who have emerged from their own suffering as stronger people. In *Amy's Last Dive*, Amy Johnson celebrates an ecstasy of achievement and liberation when she's flying solo above the seas. The more I found out about Amy the more fascinating I found her, and the more connections I could see between the confusing pressures on young women today and her brave struggles. The theme that runs through both stories is how women learn to survive and flourish after experiencing loneliness and despair. Despite the single figures at their heart, the two operas are both outstanding works of collaboration involving international artists, local residents, children and students. We've flown together and I hope that this book, as well as being a souvenir of our journey, will inspire anyone who comes across it to fly too. Look up and feel your feathers stir!

Beginnings and a plan

We pitched the idea of Wingbeats to imove in December 2009 after finding out about the possibility of funding for Yorkshire-commissioned artworks connected with the Olympics. The 'we' was a triumvirate of Adam Strickson, Alan Moir – Libraries, Arts and Heritage Group Manager for East Riding of Yorkshire Council at that time, and Matt Davison, Olympics Programmer at the University of Leeds. The proposal was revised in the early part of 2010 and officially commissioned by imove in May 2010. We formed Wingbeats Cultural Association, a constituted body with representatives from the organisations we planned to collaborate with, to oversee the delivery of the project. We then had to secure the remaining 60% of the 150K funding required to put our ideas into action. The proposal that follows describes what we planned to do. We kept closely to our original vision and programme.

Looking back at this proposal in autumn 2012, it is interesting that we describe the two main performances as 'music-theatre'. We were shy of the word 'opera', mainly because most of the members of our potential casts and audiences were unlikely ever to have attended an opera, and we thought they might be put off by the high art connotations of the word. By early 2012, we owned up and described *Amy's Last Dive* as an opera in all publicity, since we felt the exciting life of local heroine Amy Johnson was a sufficiently popular hook to attract people. And if opera, according to the Oxford Dictionary, is 'a dramatic work in one or more acts, set to music for singers and instrumentalists', then *Flight Paths* is clearly an opera too.

Curated strands proposal for imove: February 2010

Title of project: Wingbeats
Main art forms: music-theatre, creative writing/literature
Subsidiary art forms: dance, design, visual arts, film/digital imaging

Introduction

This project fits within the 'Body, Landscape and Heritage' imove strand, 're-telling the story of our physical relationship with the landscape' and 'reinterpreting our heritage in unexpected ways'. It will help people feel differently about their relationship with the moving body through an intercultural, creative encounter with the landscape and heritage of Bempton Cliffs and Flamborough Head, and with the history of flight in the East Riding.

The relationship between the moving body and the landscape is part of the area's heritage and current vitality, from the famous 'climmers' who collected seabird eggs from the cliffs while dangling on ropes to early manned flights and contemporary outdoor pursuits. The project will encourage a new relationship to the land, sea and sky of the East Riding and to Amy Johnson as an exemplum of a thinking, moving body. We will tell, re-tell and renew stories of physical relationships with the landscape through the creation of artistic experiences, re-interpreting this heritage in unexpected ways, encouraging collaboration across forms, ideas, generations and media.

Project description

The project is inspired by our perennial wish to fly and the paradoxical question: *How can we fly without leaving the ground?* It is about discovering particular stories of our physical and emotional relationship with the landscape and how imaginative movement can lead us to transcend our apparent physical limitations. It brings professional artists, university students, visitors to heritage and landscape sites, and selected youth and community participants together. It will involve an encounter with oriental movement and musical forms: Tai Chi from China and the Japanese Noh Theatre.

Over a two-and-a-half-year period, two linked music-theatre pieces will be developed through an exploration and acquired deep understanding of two specific heritage and landscape sites – Sewerby Hall, Bridlington, and its Amy Johnson collection; Flamborough Head and its birds – investigating the historical, topographical, ornithological, movement and musical connections between them.

The coast of the East Riding of Yorkshire has many associations with flying and aviation, both in the landscape and at heritage sites. The process of creating each piece will include writing, movement and music workshops, photography and film-making; physical exploration and observation of each place; performances on site and investigating relevant museum sites and collections.

Wingbeats will bring professional artists and community participants together to make innovative artworks of high quality, able to take their place on a regional and national stage. It will make links between the urban centre of Leeds and the windswept cliffs of the east coast, increasing the understanding and profile of this landscape

At the suggestion of East Riding of Yorkshire Council officers, the project will be launched to the general public with a 'Flying Day' at Sewerby Hall on July 23rd 2011, which will be a chance for thousands of people to visit Sewerby and watch or participate in thematic activities connected with the project. Possibilities include contemporary dance, African drumming from Burundi, a bird of prey demonstration, flying kites and model aeroplanes, the flight of a Gypsy Moth, singing, performances, a temporary historical exhibition about flying in the East Riding and guided walks around the area, highlighting its associations with flight.

The project will include large-scale public performances at The Spa, Bridlington, and at the University of Leeds in September 2011, and in July of the Olympic year, when we plan that the performances will be part of the Cultural Olympiad.

Flight Paths

Flight Paths, the first music-theatre performance, will take as its source the landscape and birds of Bempton Cliffs and Flamborough Head. We will observe birds on site and use the documentation of birdlife, aviation and the history of the coast in the collections of East Riding Museums as a creative resource. We will consult and involve local organisations concerned with the observation and care of the local birdlife.

We are particularly interested in how the observation of birds played a key part in the development of aviation, and how we can transfer these observations to ground-based movement and song. The composer of *Flight Paths* is Steve Kilpatrick, established contemporary composer and senior lecturer at Leeds Metropolitan University, who has recently had work performed in New York and Sweden. Parts of the composition will derive from seabird calls recorded on site.

We will collect many images and writings from workshop

participants, visitors to the area and local professional artists, which will be used as part of *LightWeight*, Impossible Theatre's four-metre by four-metre three-dimensional globe-shaped projections 'screen', which will form the design centre of both the final performance and smaller performances/exhibitions at outdoor sites.

Amy's Last Dive

The second music-theatre piece, *Amy's Last Dive*, will be based on the last part of the life of Amy Johnson, the famous Hull aviator who opened Sewerby Hall, Bridlington. Sewerby is a well known day out for Bridlington residents and visitors, and is owned by East Riding of Yorkshire Council, which is actively developing it as a landscape and heritage attraction. It is a place where land, sea and sky meet, and is famous for its evocative Amy Johnson collection. Amy opened the hall in 1936, after it had been purchased by Bridlington Corporation in 1934. Her collection of flying memorabilia was presented to Sewerby by her father in 1958 and is on display in a spectacularly elegant museum case. Amy Johnson has many associations with Hull and Bridlington, and may have first caught the flying bug in the East Riding.

Poems and Songs

The three miles of sheer cliffs at Bempton are the most amazing wildlife spectacle, comparable in their impact to an African reserve. The cliffs are packed with thousands of breeding gannets, guillemots, razorbills, kittiwakes, puffins, fulmars and shags. The seabirds start to arrive in February and by the end of April 200,000 are courting, bickering over nesting spots and hunting for fish out at sea.

The orchid-dotted meadows at the top of the cliffs provide a haven for warblers, buntings and other migratory songbirds that sing vigorously during spring and summer.

The very first workshop for Wingbeats in August 2010 took place at RSPB Bempton Cliffs, where I worked with a group of parents and children looking at the seabirds. We wrote short poems using specially prepared magnetic poetry boards with selections of words to inspire their descriptions of the birds and the landscape. Here is a selection from the playful, meditative writing produced:

Gannet's lookout
over rock avenue.
Hear her cry
in the evening –
shrill sounds.

Poppy Capes

Brambles and thistles I see
and millions of little white dots.
The wide blue sea I see
and white crumbled cliff tops.
The cycle of life I see
and I am here
and I am me.

Helen Matthews

Cliff

Grassy head
Long white dress
Feet washed
by lapping waves below.

Janet Martin

A lovely day

View together
spread coast
elaborate heights
    after
dance spray

Thousand diamond
sea ground
    after
power heave
chick feed
stare   scream.

Harold Bushby

On our walk
I saw scuttling beetles
fluttering butterflies
swooping gannets
on the layers of rock.
I saw black feathers
white feathers
fluffy feathers
speckled feathers
white dots on the waves.
I saw sunflowers
shining through.

Freddie Capes

The delicate fish
would always worship me
and nature's beauty.

Freya Hough

Webbed gannets dive for fish from the cliff and sky
where others beat their wings and chicks cry.

Nathan Hough

Fast wings beat
the music of birds.

Helen Matthews

I found that first workshop influenced my work on the first opera, *Flight Paths* or *Hope is the thing with feathers*. The combination of playful observation and deeper thoughts opened a door. I began to write poems as a preparation for working on the libretto, beginning with reflections on single seabirds, juxtaposing images that might at first seem unusual partners. The first poem I wrote, naturally enough, was about the gannets. These spectacular creatures are the glory of Bempton Cliffs, the dominant smell of the reserve in summer and Europe's largest breeding seabird. They nest side by side, with just enough room to touch each other's beaks. They plunge-dive, folding their wings right back just before they hit the water. Gannets mate for life; at Bempton, pair 33, Peckster and Flip, are the first to return every year.

In the flash company of gannets

I almost hear brass bells jangle in the wind.
With no fear, they heave above the cliff edge
like bulky Morris dancers, wave and tuck
vast hankies of wings, all graft and attitude,
raucously proud of their brash tradition.

Cult figures, less trendy than puffins
but grittier, more Manchester, the hard stuff
pogoing in hope of free food and booze,
their mosh-pit yells like rocks cracked
between capped teeth, amplified to the max.

Air bags in their dagger heads, they dive,
scoop up silver for the brat, that single chick
left in the crumbling back to back, stranded
between bar brawls – those ledge scraps
when mum or dad draw blood, or bleed.

Catch these punchy originals live –
they're the real stunting beast, icons
with centuries of cliff clings to their name;
no thought, but being, repeating this rite –
rise, fold wings
                   drop like white darkness, vanish.

The kittiwake is a beautiful, raucous small gull with a dull black zigzag on its upper wing, that nests in huge colonies at Bempton. They can often be seen in 'rafts' of hundreds of birds together sitting on the sea. In recent years, 'kitts' have begun to nest inland. In my poem about them, I explicitly link the centre of Leeds to the coast, as the story of *Flight Paths* did later. Steve Kilpatrick, the composer, was much taken with the sound of the kittiwakes and set my poem about them to music. This piece was inspired by his cacophonous recordings of the seabirds in the summer of 2010.

Voice, cry, call

Imagine if they invaded Leeds in March,
made The Headrow their cliff face,
cemented nests on every ledge –
how you'd never hear yourself speak
above their din, truckloads of sound
emptied out on every corner.

Crackled bicker of shriek –
kitt-ee-wake, kitt-ee-wake, kitt-ee-wake -
every car alarm in the multi-storey
triggered, echoing the concrete floors
while the flocks scrawl KITTS RULE
in guano on every wall and lift door.

You'd soon become desperate for August
when the thousands would take off,
cross the ring road and cooling towers,
head off over the Wolds to the coast,
fly over a lad in a wetsuit who teeters
on a ledge at Flamborough Head.

They'd head out to the North Sea,
beat off the slap of rough storm.
They'd scrape their un-rosined bows
across the growl and snarl of waves
while we cleaned the stink from the city
and learned to talk human again.

The puffin is the famously cute bird of Bempton Cliffs, with a powerful, hooked bill designed to hold slippery prey. They nest in burrows or under small rocky overhangs and have a strange, growling call, like a creaky floorboard.

'Little brother of the north'

He sleeps on the sea and sits on the sea
before he enters our overly flappy tale
of how we sought and found the holy grail
of cuteness whose creaky floorboard melody
would disgrace a cow, whose nose-job,
hookily orange in a parroty sort of way,
bench-clamps the slippery, silvery prey
he stacks and stacks in his larder of a gob.

But what's not to love in a feathered chimp,
a slack-rope walker of the air, an imp;
a faultlessly engineered, freaky sprite
whose quirky bodywork belies the quality

of calcium and keratin technology
required for sandeel-lethal, swimming flight.

One of the sources for the work we looked at was a black and white 1913 film from the Yorkshire Film Archive about the famous 'climmers' who collected seabird eggs from the cliffs in baskets while dangling on ropes. We used the film on the *LightWeight* projection structure so it was seen on sites where the climmers had worked, gathering eggs for food and for collectors. Their main prize was the pale green guillemots' eggs. With their long dagger beaks and tailcoats, 'gillies' waddle like penguins. They are strong flyers but lack agility, so landing at the nest site can sometimes take more than one attempt!

Climmer

Bempton born, a lad of twelve
has no choice but the slow lowering.

Jackdaw scrawny, cap stuffed with straw,
he takes his first turn down the cliff.

He jerks and jounces in the ropes
past the gannets' Luddite riot

past a dapperness of puffins
to the clockwork flap of guillemots.

Eyes screwed up against the wind
he swings in, fumbles out an egg

which breaks in his gawky hand
like a tater too long in a bonfire.

He licks the drips of fishy slime,
watches eggshell drift like feathers

before he swings in again and this time
comes home with his single spoil –

pale green, pear-shaped, fishy-yolked,
veined like a chart of sea depths.

His holler rings the gurling air
like a flick on the rim of a teacup

before he tugs for the pull back up
and the josh and slap of men

who basket this first of thousands
with the wick sureness of weasels.

*

That night as he lies in his bed
the sea swashes beneath him

and his clawked hands sting
where rock and beaks flayed

but he eases down in blackness,
tucks egg after egg into his bag

swinging out, swinging in –
curve of a shooting star.

This poem is about a familiar seaside and inland bird. It utters long 'aahoo' calls and deep, chuckling notes. It will eat almost anything and can be very aggressive, especially if you are eating a bag of chips! Can you guess what it is yet?

This unmentionable bird

Chip swiper, lamp post percher,
landfill scrounger, sea wall lounger,
offal scoffer, worm charmer,
rooftop yodeller, sky screamer.

It's easy to describe this bird,
the harbour bully with Doc Marten feet
in dirty pink, and mugging beak.

But we could talk about bone structure:
the way its flatfish cranium meets
the whetted knife of its beak.
Or precise wonders of form
like the red spot on its beak's underside;
a doorbell contrived for a hungry chick.

We could look for eternal truths:
the future in its right wing, the past in its left
and how it always flies in the present.

Or how it's always there
when we must go down to the sea again
and never leaves us lonely.

Like all of us, it's complex
and full of contradictions:
care and cruelty, pest and perfection,
clamour and silence.

So let's watch the flap and twist of its wings,
enjoy its yelps and barks, its head flicks,
its speckled chicks, the way it claws the air
above spilt cornets and plastic chairs.

For this unmentionable one is a bard's bird,
with us from plough and hallow
to webcam and disgorging cities, soaring
from the alliterative heave of the Saxon sea
to the jagged coast of this arcade poem.

Oh egg stealer, crab smasher,
bin bag ripper, boat-lake sipper,
stiff stepper, beach cleaner,
thermal drifter, dive-bomber,
let's raise a cup of mead to your gull-ness
and prepare a feast of battered herring.

One of my birdwatching friends calls all those small birds that are so difficult to identify 'sbjs' (small brown jobbies). I was lucky enough to spend time with Steve Race, the photographer and Outreach Officer at Bempton Cliffs, who pointed out the wonder of these birds and let me look at them through his scope. The meadows at Bempton 'hide' many small birds, and these became the 'farm birds' of the opera.

Small brown birdness

Locustella, loper, hopper and creeper, skulker,
'Gropper', Grasshopper Warbler flitters, whirrs.

Then beak opens to reel out ticking call.

My eye adjusts to mouse-smallness in scope lens
and follows a tap-dance up hogweed stem.

Freewheelin' boarder. Blast-off jink.
Brownness blue as the sea.

Saharan speck. Next year's slip-in.

Three songs from *Spitfire Irene*

During the time I was working on *Flight Paths*, I also completed a song cycle, set to music by Edward Caine, who played the keyboard for *Amy's Last Dive*. He set the words for unaccompanied soprano voice, including a large variety of plane noises! Both Peyee Chen and Lizzie Marshall sang the work during the project, at the Howard Assembly Room in Leeds and Sewerby Hall respectively. *Spitfire Irene* was inspired by Schumann and Chamisso's *Frauenliebe und leben* ('A Woman's Love and Life'). It brings to life seven moments from the long life of Irene, who was an ATA (Air Transport Auxiliary) woman pilot during World War II. These brave women flew unarmed, without radios or instruments, to deliver planes to male pilots who flew them into battle. This was Amy Johnson's job at the time of her death. Irene's story is fictional but firmly based on fact. Like many women who took on 'male' jobs in the war, her subsequent life was something of a disappointment; no love for a man ever compared with the thrill of flying a Spitfire. In 2011, at the age of ninety, she has reached a profound understanding of her journey, and, deep inside, knows she is still flying. Irene became a character in *Flight Paths*.

2.

Darling of the air

>Convent school.
>'Doing an Amy'.
>Stuck out my arms.
>Flew across the quad.

I was a darling of the air.

Flying lessons.
Went solo.
Took a Tiger high.
Played with clouds.

I was a darling of the air.

War. Joined up.
Air Transport Auxiliary.
Ferried planes to men.
Risked neck.

I was a darling of the air.

Flew unarmed.
No radio. No instruments.
Frontline delivery.
Loved every moment.

I was a darling of the air.

3.

You moved. I moved.

You moved. I moved.
My glorious Spitfire.
How snug! How thrilling!
The tremor in your wings!

You moved. I moved.
My Spit... spit... fire!

With my swept-back curls
I was your Attagirl!

You moved. I moved.
My Spitter! My fire!
Your metal loveliness
trembled with eagerness!

*

Perhaps it was never meant
that I learnt to feel free inside you.

You moved. I moved.

How I learnt to feel free inside you!

7.

Woman much missed.

Oh Wendy girl, Attagirl,
Spitter girl, sky-high girl

Woman much missed
how you call to me
call to me

I'm ninety now, ninety, ninety!

When I pluck the sparrow's tail,
I feel my six-stone body fail
but woolly sleeves hide hidden wings
and deep inside a bird still sings.

I'm ninety now, ninety, ninety!

Oh Wendy girl, Attagirl,
Spitter girl, sky-high girl

Woman much missed
how you call to me
call to me
call to me

FLIGHT PATHS

or

HOPE IS THE THING WITH FEATHERS

2011

Birds, women, and writing

The titles

The title *Flight Paths* first appeared because I needed a title for the original proposal. It has connotations of aeroplanes, migratory birds and – by implication – the different routes we might take in life. Towards the end of work on the libretto I was reading Emily Dickinson's poems again. She is a writer I regularly return to, loving the mixture of exploratory freedom and containment found in her small mysterious poems. 'Hope is the thing with feathers' is poem number 254 from her life's work and this phrase seemed to express succinctly the idea of finding renewal in the natural world that is such an important part of Erin's journey:

> "Hope" is the thing with feathers
> That perches in the soul

The story

Hope is the thing with feathers is the story of two 'flying' journeys, an inner journey of self-discovery and an outer journey along an amazing coast. The events take place on a walk between Bempton Cliffs and Flamborough on midsummer's day 2011, and are based on the lives of real people.

At the beginning, the choir repeat the words 'Missing despondent female', taken from a Flamborough coastguard's report. Our 'despondent female' is Erin, a young African-Caribbean university student from Leeds with a two-year-old daughter. Her mother, who looks after the little girl, has become very ill and Erin will have to give up her studies. In a moment of despair, she remembers a caravan park where she once spent a holiday with her mum. She heads for the coast to end it all. But when she arrives at Bempton Cliffs she finds cars, hundreds of people and thousands of seabirds. Heading for the cliff edge, she literally runs into Ilona, an RSPB guide, who starts her on a rollercoaster journey of encounters with birdlife and people on the coastal path. She meets kittiwakes, gannets, farm birds and peregrines. She stumbles across Spitfire Irene, a ninety-year-old ex ATA (Air Transport Auxiliary) pilot who served in World War II. She is regaled by Linda, a karaoke singer on holiday at Thornwick Bay. 'Tombstoners' tempt her to jump at White Rock. She meets Vi, a lady from Haworth who lost her granddaughter to cancer. Will she be able to turn her life around by the end of the day, when she reaches South Landing beach after passing through a star of swords?

How do I begin writing? With thoughts like these –

A patch of map. Four squares of sea.
The Zen of blue.
A relationship with landscape.
Because I am human, the human in the landscape.
A blank space waiting to be filled
or an invitation to clear-headed emptiness.

Two squares of land.
A car park. A bird reserve.
A narrow, cliff path.
A lifeboat station. A farm.
A path down to the beach.

Four squares of sea.
The Zen of blue.
A beach and four squares of sea –
the setting for the end of a story.

On being inspired by a page opened at random in a loved book –

There are few dreams in books. Dreams used to occur in all the great books, then they became more remote. I associate this increasing remoteness, this desiccation, with the diminishment of other signs. In the same way we find:

> less and less poetry
> less and less angels
>
> less and less birds
> less and less women
> less and less courage.

...let the dream grow. It grows down – towards the depths.

From *Three Steps on the Ladder of Writing* (1993), Hélène Cixous, Columbia University Press, New York.

Hope is the thing with feathers grows out of poetry, includes angels, contains thousands of birds, is about women's courage and, briefly, enters the depths of the sea. Is it a dream?

Unlike my other opera libretti, this work is not an adaptation of existing material. My first writing exercise was a cliff walk in the snow and damp of winter, from mid-morning to sunset, taking photographs and making feverish notes about everything around for possible inclusion in the narrative. And of course, I had to imagine the landscape on midsummer's day 2011, which is when I had decided the action would take place. *Amy's Last Dive* is set on midwinter's eve 2011, and there is a deliberate, companionable and slightly skewed symmetry in these choices of time. These 'witching' days hold the possibility of magical, life-transforming happenings as the sun and earth mark the low and high points of the year.

Hope is the thing with feathers is an original story that takes place on a walk between two points on the East Riding coast. I have to say that writing an original story is so much more difficult than the business of adaptation; after all, most Elizabethan playwrights never wrote one and I can make an educated guess that at least 95% of operas are adaptations of existing stories. But all you need to make a story is the journey of a life through a landscape, and a structure.

Hope is the thing with feathers combines aspects of classical storytelling derived from Robert McKee's *Story* {*Story, substance, structure, style and the principles of screenwriting* (1999), Robert McKee, Methuen, London} and the hero's quest described in Christopher Vogler's inspirational *The Writer's Journey* {*The Writer's Journey, Mythic structure for writers* (1998), Christopher Vogler, Michael Weise Productions, Studio City, California}.

A response to Robert McKee's teachings on structuring a dramatic work

The principle of creative limitation

As McKee writes, the world of a story must be small enough for the writer to know every inch of the fictional universe he creates. For *Hope is the thing with feathers*, this has to be an informed knowing of names: the stones, the fields, the insects, the plants, the birds, the animals, the stiles, the gates, the beaches, the North Sea and the underwater reef, combined with a deep knowledge of the internal life of each character and everything that's ever happened to them. It has to be a walking, running, climbing, swimming, talking and flying knowledge of the actual territory, not just the map.

McKee believes all stories take place within a limited, knowable world. But this world contains the dreams and visions of the characters, their internal life as well as external events. I believe there should always be space for the unknowable within this limited world, the journey of the soul we find at the edge of our consciousness and beyond.

Kinetic events

Hope is the thing with feathers is a kinetic story: moving bodies in a landscape respond to each other and what's around them, as McKee understands –

'A storyteller is a life-poet, an artist who transforms day-to-day living, inner life and outer life, dream and actuality into *a poem whose rhyme scheme is events rather than words* – a two-hour metaphor that says: Life is like *this*!' (McKee, 2009: 25)

The structure of the opera is a selection of events or actions from a specific life story (Erin, a young woman from Leeds at a moment of crisis in her life) arranged in a sequence to arouse specific emotions. The audience is hungry to know how it feels to be alive on the knife edge of now. What does it mean to be a human being today, overcoming difficulties and challenges?

'Event' means *change*. Each event changes Erin, taking her closer to healing, whether subconsciously (in the earlier part of the narrative) or consciously.

The event-changes of the narrative are revealed through a

series of kinetic images that the writer must be able to see as a storyboard, a series of progressive pictures, in his head. The material used to draw these pictures is taken from the mind and body of a living human being acting, and being acted upon, in an actual landscape. *Hope* needs a choreographer to structure all the movement that's integral to the story – the running rush to the edge of the cliff, the flying dance of the peregrines, the elation of swimming in the cold sea and deep Tai Chi breathing on a beach as the arms of the characters move like birds' wings. The strongest kinetic images stay in our mind for ever: Lear throwing himself over the cliff to land on the hard stage at his feet; a tramp with his boot off picking his foot underneath a tree; maybe Erin running headlong into the sea at South Landing?

These pictures must exclude 90% of known reality because dramatic reality doesn't allow time and space for that level of detail. Peter Brook, as a director, and McKee, as a screenwriting theorist, both write about reworking the same images throughout and making the best use of a few objects. How many objects do we need to tell the story of *King Lear?* A map, a chair, a set of stocks, some rotting food, wild flowers, mud and some swords. And for *Hope is the thing with feathers?* A scope for looking at birds, a jar of piccalilli, a folding chair, a pack of Angel Cards and some swords.

Plot

Using McKee's understanding of plot as an analytical tool, *Hope is the thing with feathers* contains elements of archplot (CLASSICAL DESIGN: causality, linear time, single protagonist, consistent reality) and miniplot (MINIMALISM: open ending, internal conflict, passive protagonist) and a healthy sprinkling of antiplot (ANTI-STRUCTURE: coincidence, inconsistent realities, dream). McKee gives the writer permission to move anywhere within this triangle of plots, though he's in no doubt about the inherent superiority of the archplot. *Hope is the thing with feathers* looks towards a more intuitive, open structure that McKee, somewhat condescendingly, says we often find in European 'art films'.

McKee posits the idea that the art film's focus on inner conflict draws the interest of those with advanced degrees, because the inner world is where the highly educated spend a large amount of their time! But we are all extraordinary people with the potential for a rich inner life whatever our educational background. Over many years, my work in disadvantaged communities making theatre from people's life stories has revealed the truth of this again and again.

Hope has an open ending (Erin will get on with her life but for how long, and what events will challenge her next?), linear time (one walk on one specific day) and a consistent reality; it has her internal conflicts (albeit externalised or turned into metaphor), and she is a largely passive protagonist who responds to others rather than taking initiative herself. The structure makes deliberate use of coincidence – for example, the reappearance of Ilona in the sea at the end of the story, though this has the consistency of myth since the name means 'torch' and she is Erin's spiritual guide at the beginning and end of the journey.

The writer's compositional plan for a narrative-based opera rooted in the kinetic act of walking

The kinetic is our sixth sense; our awareness of how the bones, muscles and fluids of the body change as we move from one balance to another.
Kinetic = relating to or resulting from motion; (of a work of art) depending on movement for its effect.
The word comes from the Greek *kinein:* 'to move'.

Ten stages

The first stage – thought and preparation
The second stage – <u>the walk</u>, *an obviously kinetic act*
The third stage – collation, collection and reflection

The fourth stage – the exploratory writing and/or devising, *an imaginative act*
The fifth stage – the characters and the story, *an imaginative act*
The sixth stage – the plot, *an imaginative act*
The seventh stage – the script (image, words and the action), *an imaginative act*

The script meets the process of musical composition – an obviously kinetic act

The eighth stage – reanimating <u>the walk</u>; the rehearsal, *an obviously kinetic act*
The ninth stage – performance, *an obviously kinetic act*
The tenth stage – reflection, which may lead to a new first stage

But if the walk moves inside us throughout the compositional process, then all ten stages are kinetic acts. As the writer images the walk, his balance changes from moment to moment.

Extracts from a creative diary

24/9/2010

I'm going to write at least one of these a week while I'm working on the libretto, as a self-reflective supportive analysis for myself but also, hopefully, to give an insight into one evolving process of writing a script, or in this case a libretto. One of the main differences between a stage script and a libretto (the words for opera or music-theatre) is that a libretto is much sparer. Cut, cut and cut again! You also have to bear in mind that no matter how interested the composer is in words, the audience will only ever hear 60% of them.

It's as much like writing a poem as writing a script, which is one of the main reasons I'm interested in this slightly egoless process. In fact, it's a lot like writing a Japanese poem.

In scriptwriting terms, what I'm writing about here is the COLLECTION stage when you gather ideas and do the research: reading, watching, talking, interviewing, picking people's brains, taking photographs, sketching and looking at a myriad of background materials and other inspirations which gradually sift down. It's often the longest stage, though definitely not the hardest. It's probably the most enjoyable time, apart from that feeling of having the first completed draft printed out on pristine white paper.

It must be six months since I had my initial ideas and longer since I decided the general theme for this first of two music-theatre pieces: the birds and landscape of Bempton Cliffs and Flamborough Head. I spent a couple of days with Steve Race of the RSPB in the summer. On the second day in August we did an observation and writing workshop with two groups of adults and children, largely responding to the landscape and to the gannets, since most of the other breeding birds had left by then. A few bits of writing done on that day, especially the one below, written by a woman who came with her young child, helped towards my thoughts about the narrative for the piece –

> As the water beneath
> lights a moment
> I stop   I sit
> time is not there
>
> Helen Matthews

This led to me thinking about Bempton Cliffs as a different kind of space in life, a place of transition, a stop along the journey which might change you for ever – and a space where time operates in a different way from everyday life.

There's a quotation on all the RSPB poster boards at Bempton which connected with this –

> 'It was sanctuary from the city, from clouds of exhaust fumes, from anger, from drudgery – not just for the birds – for me and my little girl.'
>
> Simon Franks

These two brief sets of words set me thinking about the journey from the city to the country, from Leeds to Bridlington to Bempton Cliffs, and why someone might make that journey, and how it might change them. I thought of getting there by public transport: a bus or a walk, the slow train to Brid and then a bus out to Flamborough or Bempton and another walk…and maybe a dive and a swim. All moving, all exercise…all steps on a journey, and maybe – metaphorically – a walking towards flight.

The kinetic question behind the project is, 'How can we fly

without leaving the ground?' and I've been thinking of a central character who needs to learn to 'take off' in her life, and who sees all sorts of different experiences of 'flying on the ground' and actual flying on her journey towards her own 'flight'.

Running, leaping, jumping into the sea from a cliff ledge, swimming underwater, throwing yourself into the long grass in a cliff meadow and rolling, dancing on the beach, walking into pitch darkness – all these are kinds of 'flying' in physical movement. They're all about 'leaving the ground' in some way.

25/9/2010

I'm wrestling with STRUCTURE (the second stage) and looking at seemingly contradictory sources and guidelines to achieve this. It is the really difficult part of the process, especially when it is an original story. So much of my script work is adaptation, either stated or 'secret' and disguised. This isn't, so for help with structure I'm looking at:

- *The Hero's Journey* or Quest Structure (a la Joseph Campbell and Christopher Vogler). This is actually what I started with to make some sense of some very disparate material.

- Robert McKee's understanding of the conventional three-act-structure but with a nod to two-act-structures, which are really a condensation and slight simplification of the three-act structure.

- A seemingly contradictory source: Maya Deren's films, which are what McKee calls 'anti-structure', especially *At Land*. This source is a bridge between structure and content.

- The nature of the space for the main performances, the huge, domed ballroom of The Spa, Bridlington, where different parts of the audience will see things from below and above – multiple and differing audience perspectives.

For content (which is, in essence, my COLLECTION), this is the eccentric list I am drawing on so far:

- The site itself. The drama will take place over a period from around 9.30am in the morning to twilight in the area between Bempton Cliffs and the South Landing at Flamborough, a distance of 11 miles. This is a sort of conforming to the dramatic unities and both digital and drawn/painted images will illustrate and counterpoint this journey. I'm exploring all dimensions: the sky above, the cliffs, the meadows, the path and under the sea. I need to go and walk these 11 miles as soon as possible. There is a photographic diary of this walk on the net, and a series of Google Earth images on the same route contributed by different people.

- The history of aviation in the area, especially RAF Bempton and the Air Transport Auxiliary in the Second World War (some of whom were women).

    This may mean some research through interviews as well as the web, to bring what I need from the story to life. Sherburn-in-Elmet between Leeds and York was one of the ferry airports for delivery.

- Online videos about 'tombstoning' (jumping off cliffs) at Flamborough. Articles about the same and the posh version – 'coasteering'.

- Doug Johnstone's 2006 novel *Tombstoning*, which

only touches on the world of tombstoners but is a useful and gripping piece of plotting around small, bleak, seaside-town hopes and aspirations, and the threat and availability of a huge cliff for murder and suicide. Reading this also persuaded me to keep away from the ex-soldier motif which, with Iraq and Afghanistan, is all too tempting.

- Photographs and films of the birds at Bempton and Flamborough.

- Natural history books on seabirds and the area.

- The information board at South Landing about the underwater life.

- An early film from the Yorkshire Film Archive of the 'climmers' at Jubilee Corner at Bempton Cliffs (1913).

- The fruits of a writing workshop for adults and children in August 2010 – short poems and found pieces based on magnetic poetry.

- My own exploratory poems about seabirds and climming at Bempton, written since the August workshop day. The poems link urban imagery with the birds.

- Local musical traditions: Jim Eldon, fiddler and singer on the boat out from Bridlington every summer, and the Flamborough Longsword Dancers.

- The song *Shoals of Herring*.

- Web stuff on the 'Flamborough Trolls' and the temporary 'pagan' sculptures in the area.

- The Anglo-Saxon poem, *The Seafarer*.

- Other short poems, like Norman MacCaig's on a puffin and Mary Oliver's on gannets.

- The local bus timetable from Bridlington to the coast.
- The project publicity image: a young woman disappearing into the sea next to Bempton Cliffs.
- John Burnside's GRANTA article 'How to Fly', about learning to fly as a child and all the pilots who vanished in the early history of aviation right up to the Second World War.
- Noel Coward songs – for the ATA woman character.
- The Yorkshire Birdman, and other birdmen.
- Maya Deren's dance films.
- Tarkovsky's film *Stalker*, especially the general concept of the 'Zone'. The 'Zone' grants the deepest innermost wishes of anyone who steps inside. Perhaps the whole site is a 'zone' and 'time is not there', as Helen Matthews wrote in her poem.
- The philosophical, meditative poetry used in *Stalker*, by Fyodor Tyutchev.
- The main character's attempts to fly in Lorrie Moore's novel *A Gate at the Stairs*.
- David Nash's sculpture – especially the larger sets of three forms, and the exhibition at Yorkshire Sculpture Park, 2010–11.
- The ability to use Impossible Theatre's *LightWeight* 4m x 4m projection 'globe' installation for still and animated contemporary and archive images to counterpoint the action.
- Being at the edge of things – a description from A S Byatt's *The Children's Book* of how we see the world as a globe where sea meets land.

- A performance I saw in Dartington Great Hall, south Devon, many years ago when the only set was the huge wooden table.

- Older people – really old (88+) being able to dance, and a film I saw a long time ago about a group of old men dancing in Canada, which was very moving.

- The relentless, weight-dragging circular journeys with baggage around the stage, accompanied by repetitive waltzes, in some of Tadeusz Kantor's theatre work – a parallel to the relentless attempts of man to fly with all sorts of different devices.

- J. A. Baker's *The Peregrine* – one of the most beautiful and perceptive wildlife books ever, about one type of bird in one location.

- Staying in B&Bs in Bridlington, especially the small single rooms.

- What I already have of Steve Kilpatrick's previous music and talking with him about the raucousness of the seabirds at Bempton Cliffs, how there is no sweetness in their calls.

- 'Doing an Amy', i.e. flying around the school playground with your arms out.

- Images from the film *The Last Tightrope Dancers of Armenia*.

Flight Paths or *Hope is the thing with feathers*

a Wingbeats performance, was commissioned by imove and formed part of the Cultural Olympiad. It was premiered on the 24th September 2011 at The Spa, Bridlington.

Three further performances took place at The Spa on the 25th September and on the 1st October at stage@leeds, University of Leeds.

WRITTEN AND DIRECTED BY Adam Strickson
COMPOSED BY Steve Kilpatrick

MUSICAL DIRECTOR: Jonathan Lo
CHOIR LEADER: Em Whitfield-Brooks
CHOREOGRAPHER: Balbir Singh
DESIGNER: Jane Robinson
LIGHTWEIGHT DESIGN AND OPERATION: Chris Squire & Impossible Theatre
LIGHTING DESIGN: Paul Halgarth
DESIGN COLLABORATORS: Vivien Mousdell & Sarah Riley
STAGE MANAGER: James Thompson

WINGBEATS PROJECT DIRECTOR: Lara Goodband
WINGBEATS PRODUCER FOR IMOVE: Jenny Harris

Cast

ERIN, a young woman from Leeds: Nadine Mortimer-Smith
ILONA, an RSPB guide at Bempton Cliffs
and LINDA, a holidaymaker: Aniko Toth
SPITFIRE IRENE, a ninety-year-old ex-Second World War pilot
and VI, a Yorkshire grandmother: Taylor Wilson

Tombstoners

SEAN: Jon Neaves
NINER: Mikey McCulloch
CATTEE: Georgia Mason

Musicians

Erik Peterson, Emily Ondracek-Peterson,
Ilya Movchan, Alisa Liubarskaya (Voxare Quartet)

Bridlington Community Chorus

Jane Winn, Jessica Sinclair, Margaret Croft, Sally Wilkinson, Sheila Cadman, Stephanie Naylor, Patricia Holroyd, Wendy Harrison, Ann Hatfield, Anne Parr, Barbara Birtle, Beverley Fieldhouse, Dinah Western, Gill Kay, Gille Andrews

Buckrose Concert Band

CONDUCTOR: Rebecca Heywood

Bird dancers

Charlotte Fisher, Samantha Broadbent, Josie McCartney (Balbir Singh Dance Company)
Leyla Carter, Leah Pejica, Charlotte North (School of PCI, University of Leeds)
Katey Poutch (East Riding Youth Dance Company)

Farm birds

Flamborough CE Primary School Years 4 & 5 (in Bridlington)
Lindley Junior School Choir (in Leeds)

FLIGHT

PATHS

or

HOPE IS THE

THING WITH

FEATHERS

Characters

ERIN
an African-Caribbean young woman from Leeds, aged 23

ILONA
an RSPB guide at Bempton Cliffs, originally from Hungary, in her early thirties

SPITFIRE IRENE
a ninety-year-old ex-Second World War pilot who served in the ATA

LINDA
a holidaymaker and keen karaoke singer, in her late thirties

VI
a Yorkshire grandmother in her mid-seventies

SEABIRDS (Dancers)

A PAIR OF PEREGRINES (Dancers)

FARM BIRDS (A chorus of children)

TOMBSTONERS
Sean and Niner, aged 17; Cattee, Sean's girlfriend, aged 16

PROLOGUE

'The city' – images of inner Leeds.

THE CHOIR sing *(very quietly)*: Just a crow. Corvus corone. Azzuro-negro.

The other two soloists echo the words of the song under ERIN's melody.

ERIN: A crow flew into my window, my city window.

> Just a crow and you shouldn't blame a crow
> but next day I came home and found my mum out cold.
>
> I have a gorgeous daughter who's two years old.
> While I studied hard, my mum cared for her,
> played with her, gave all her precious time to her.
>
> Then a crow flew into my window, my city window.
>
> Just a crow and you shouldn't blame a crow
> but my dancing mum has grown suddenly old.
>
> Now my precious time has gone, my life's been sold
> to someone I don't know, who just can't cope –
> this stuck-at-home girl who's lost all hope.
>
> A crow flew into my window, my city window.
> Now that crow's leading me out of my life.
>
> Just a crow and you shouldn't blame a crow
> for helping me to fly beautifully out of my life.

ERIN runs off.

Overture

The seabirds dance, and – towards the end of the overture – the suggestion of a crow dances.

ACT 1

SCENE 1

Midsummer's Day 2011, Bempton Cliffs.

The seabirds continue to dance. ILONA *stands on the cliffs, dressed in her RSPB uniform, with a birdwatching scope on a stand.*

ILONA: Two hundred thousand birds.

Bempton Cliffs.   Seabird city.

This is our Serengeti.

This is our life on earth.

Gannet chorus

SOLOISTS: Sea-sounding sea   and gannets' shanty.

ILONA: Gannet crag   gannet pile   gannet plunge.

CHOIR: (A) Arrah Arr Urrah *(A barking sound)*

(B) Gannet creech   gannet pother   gannet cry.

ILONA: Two hundred thousand birds.

Bempton Cliffs.   Seabird city.

This is our Serengeti.

This is our life on earth.

Gannet chorus

SOLOISTS: Sea sounding sea   and gannets' shanty.

ILONA: Gannet crag   gannet pile   gannet plunge.

CHOIR: (A) Arrah Arr Urrah *(A barking sound)*

(B) Gannet creech   gannet pother   gannet cry.

ERIN reappears, running towards the cliff. She is breathless. Her words are fragmented and cut through the chorus; sometimes the chorus suddenly stops, leaving her words surrounded by silence. Her first line is shouted out.

ERIN: Gonna reach those cliffs   an' fly out of my life

fly so beautifully out of my life   out of my life

She runs into ILONA, who instinctively grabs her.

ERIN: Take your hands off me!

Leave me alone.

Sorry   I'm so sorry   I didn't mean –

ILONA: Calm down. Look... down.

ILONA turns ERIN around. The seabirds fill the space. They rise and fall, with a great deal of noise.

ERIN: Oh my God! Thousands!

Thousands and thousands!

ILONA: Kitts kittiwakes calling their own name

(Two parts, A & B, sung simultaneously.)

SOLOISTS: *(A)* Kitt-ee-wake, kitt-ee-wake, kitt-ee-wake

Crackled/bicker/of shriek

(B) Missing despondent female,
missing despondent female

kitt-ee-wake, kitt-ee-wake, kitt-ee-wake

They continue, under ERIN's words.

ERIN: It's like... Saturday!

Like Elland Road... the North Stand...

the noisiest stand

the North Stand... the noisiest stand

My Dad used to take me... when I was little

my Dad used to take me... on Saturday

(ERIN:)	the North Stand… the noisiest stand
CHOIR:	Kitt-ee-wake, kitt-ee-wake, kitt-ee-wake
(Quietly)	Missing despondent female, missing despondent female
	Kitt-ee-wake, kitt-ee-wake, kitt-ee-wake
ERIN:	I need to go now.
ILONA:	I'll walk with you.
ERIN:	No –
ILONA:	I'll walk with you.

SCENE 2

Walk music. ERIN *is pulling away from* ILONA, *who carries the scope on its stand.* ILONA *puts the scope down, focuses it and beckons* ERIN *to look. At first* ERIN *refuses but curiosity gets the better of her.* ILONA *sings a descant to the song above the melody.*

FARM BIRDS & ILONA:	Legs of twig and eyes of seeds, beaks of flint and wings of reeds. Legs of twig and eyes of seeds, beaks of flint and wings of reeds.
ILONA:	What can you see?
ERIN:	Nothing. Just… grass!

ILONA: Look. Listen.

FARM BIRDS　　Hid among the grasses there
& ILONA:　　　our hidden voices haunt the air.
　　　　　　　You may see us if you hush:
　　　　　　　skylark, warbler, thrush.

　　　　　　　We're woodcocks in the tree tops
　　　　　　　who scatter if you sneeze.
　　　　　　　We're buntings on the fence posts
　　　　　　　who sound like jangling keys.

　　　　　　　We're agile crested lapwings
　　　　　　　rising up with ease.
　　　　　　　We're yellow-feathered siskins
　　　　　　　wheezing in the breeze.

　　　　　　　Hid among the grasses there
　　　　　　　our hidden voices haunt the air.
　　　　　　　You can see us if you hush:
　　　　　　　skylark, warbler, thrush.

FARM BIRD: Tseek-tseek-tseek-tississisk

　　　　　　Tseek-tseek-tseek-tississisk

This call continues until the reed bunting flies up.

ILONA: A reed bunting! On top of that teasel.

　　　　　Pause.

　　　　　It's got a black and white head.

　　　　　It looks like it's been dipped in rust.

ERIN:	Amazing! Beautiful!
	Pause, as she watches it.
	Oh, it's gone. It's flown away.
	It was hidden… alone.
	Just like a tuft of grass.
ILONA:	There's so much we don't see.
	Pause.
	What's your name?
ERIN: *(Spoken)*	I told you to leave me alone.

	Pause.	(ERIN: *very quietly*) hidden… alone
ILONA:	My name's Ilona. I work here.	
		(ERIN: *very quietly*) just like a tuft of grass
	I help people	show them the birds.
(Sung)	Two hundred thousand birds.	

Pause. Then ILONA *picks up the scope.*

ERIN: *(Spoken)*	My name is Erin.

ILONA: Erin. And you're from Leeds?

ERIN: Leave me alone.

Pause.

ILONA: Look, let me give you my phone number.

ERIN *searches her pockets.*

ERIN: I must have dropped my phone...on the road.

I'll be alright... I'm not your problem.

ERIN *walks away quickly along the cliff path and then freezes in mid-motion.*

ILONA:
(Sung) Look up there! Our peregrines.

Our deadly falcons.

The rippling slash of wings!

You'll see feathers on the path.

All that's left of pigeons.

Feathers on the path.

Our lithe and thrilling peregrines!

So large, and shining.

(ILONA:)   So large, and shining.

Peregrine dance

(Spoken)   Follow them, Erin.   Please follow them.

SCENE 3

(Walk music). *Between Wandale Nab and Cat Nab.*

Solo

ERIN: When I was a little girl in Woodhouse, Leeds,
my window framed a city park
of burning tyres and broken glass.

When I was a bigger girl in Cookridge, Leeds,
my window framed a leafy wood
of walks with mum and chattering birds.

Now I am a grown-up girl and still in Leeds,
my window frames a skip piled high
with broken hopes and burning fears.

Broken hopes and burning fears!

Gonna reach those cliffs   an' fly outta my life

fly so beautifully out of my life   outta my life

She psyches herself up. She runs. She teeters on the edge of the cliff. The choir sing kitt-ee-wake, kitt-ee-wake, kitt-ee-wake *very softly.*

(ERIN:)	Stand still! Stand still!
	So far down so far to fly.

ACT 2

SCENE 1

Between Wandale Nab and Cat Nab.

ERIN is distracted by the appearance of IRENE, who is sitting in a deckchair having a picnic. IRENE suddenly stands up.

IRENE:	*(She sings the first verse of Noel Coward's 'I'll see you again'.)*
	Ham and piccalilli, dear? A glass of wine?
ERIN:	You're mad.
IRENE: *(Spoken)*	Very likely, dear.
	Pause.
(Sung)	As they say on the TV, I'm Irene and I'm ninety!
	I was a wife, twice. I am a mother, once.
	But I'm dancing and singing in the sun and looking forward to ninety-one.

(IRENE:) I live my life one day at a time. I was a Spitfire pilot.

ERIN: A Spitfire pilot!

IRENE: Flew over these cliffs in forty-one

in my Spit/my Spitter/my Spit-fire!

ERIN: Your Spitfire?

IRENE: It moved. I moved. I've never felt so free.

She flies like a plane.

It moved. I moved. I've never felt so free.

I was an Attagirl with swept-back curls.

I was an Attagirl!

ERIN: You were an Attagirl!

Pause.

IRENE: Attagirls! Attagirls!

We delivered planes.

Flew over these cliffs in forty-one
in my Spit/my Spitter/my Spit-fire!

ERIN: Your Spitfire?

IRENE: Attagirls! Attagirls!

(IRENE:) We never felt the same.
We delivered planes,
flew them to the frontline,
flew them to the brave boys
who flew them into battle,
battle, battle.

Hurricanes, Lancasters,
Barracudas. Spit, spit, spitfires.

Attagirls! Attagirls!
We delivered planes.
We never felt the same.

Oh we were astonishingly brave girls,
the brave girls who played with the clouds.

She does the Tai Chi movement 'Wave hands like clouds'.

ERIN:
(*Spoken*) What are you doing?

IRENE: Wave hands like clouds. Wave hands like clouds.

Tai Chi.

(*Sung*) I keep on flying.

She performs another Tai Chi movement.

(*Spoken*) Owwww, my knees. My poor old knees.

Pause.

(IRENE:)   You were going to jump, jump from the cliffs.

   Pause.

ERIN:
(Sung)   Why can't I be a little girl
   in a caravan by the sea?
   With water wings,
   shells and swings
   and always chips for tea.

   Why can't I be a little girl
   in a caravan by the sea.
   Those rock-pool days
   with sand and spade,
   just my mum and me.

These lines and IRENE*'s overlap and repeat as a duet.*

   It's like... I'm blinded by my life.
   I don't want my life.

   I'm blinded by my life.

IRENE: No one sends you   another life!

   Look at me. Look at me!

   My best friend killed at twenty.

   My first husband left me.

   My second died at thirty.

   But I'm still flying free

(IRENE:)　　　　and playing with the clouds.

(Spoken)　　　Promise me –

ERIN:　　　　　Promise you what?

IRENE:　　　　 Get through it.　Women get through it.

　　　　　　　　We are astonishingly brave girls.

　　　　　　　　Promise me.

　　　　　　　　Pause.

　　　　　　　　Promise me.

ERIN:
(Quietly)　　　I promise.

　　　　　　　　She continues walking.

IRENE:　　　　 Goodbye, then.

(Sung)　　　　If she could just stand on top of the cliff,
　　　　　　　　look out, look down, somehow feel the curve...

　　　　　　　　As she is singing, her moving hands describe a large ball shape.

　　　　　　　　of the huge, flying ball
　　　　　　　　the watery, wonderful earth
　　　　　　　　the grey and rainbow sky
　　　　　　　　turning, spinning, living!

SCENE 2

Walk music. *Dyke's End to Gull Nook.*

ERIN:
(Spoken)   I promise nothing.

(Sung)   Feathers on the path.

She picks up the feathers and turns them over in her hand. Peregrine dance music begins.

            What did Ilona call those birds?

            Deadly falcons. Pe-re-grines.

(Shouted)   Finish me off, you murder birds!

Peregrine dance

            Pause.

            When I was a little girl,
            mum was a caterpillar butterfly
            and I was her pretty little dragonfly
            dancin' and jumpin' all day long.

            She laughs.

(Spoken)   Dancin' on carnival day
            in sunny Chapeltown!
            'Jump if you jumpin!!'
            'Jump if you jumpin!!'

            She cries.

SCENE 3

Walk music. ERIN *continues her walk.*

ERIN:
(Spoken)   A holiday park! Caravans!
Loads of green caravans.

              I know our caravan was somewhere around here.

The wind band come on stage dressed in holiday gear, in puffin colours. LINDA *brings on a garish deckchair and drinks from a can of beer.*

LINDA:
(Sung)   You've picked a lovely day for a walk, dear.

             Where have you come from?

ERIN:
(Spoken)   Leeds.

LINDA: Eeee Leeds, like it or lump it!

             We're from Donny. Doncaster!

(Sung)   And where have you come from today?

ERIN:
(Spoken)   Ur... Bempton Cliffs.

LINDA:
(Sung)   Did you see the puffins?

Short puffin piece. *It refers to the melody of 'When a Felon's not Engaged in his Employment' from* The Pirates of Penzance *and includes cow-like puffin noises and, possibly, puffin movements. Words from* CHOIR:

Puffin/puffin/puffin/puffin/puffin/puffin/puffin/puffin/ /Mad Clown/Sea Parrot/Fratercula Arcticula/Little Brother of the North/Pulcinella di Mare/Macareux Moine/ /Puffin/puffin/puffin/puffin/puffin/puffin/puffin/puffin.

LINDA:
(Sings)   Ooooooh, yesterday we went to see the puffins

CHOIR: see the puffins

LINDA: And a puffin has got really flappy feet

CHOIR: flappy feet

LINDA: They whizz about like they've got outboard motors

CHOIR: outboard motors

LINDA: And all the kiddies laugh when they're around

CHOIR: they're around

Repeat of the puffin piece

LINDA:
(Spoken)   Do you like music?

ERIN: Yeah, R & B. I used to like the Spice Girls.

LINDA: I like all sorts. And I'm a devil for the karaoke.

(She sings the first verse of 'The Wind Beneath My Wings')

(Spoken) Ooooh The Divine Miss M.
Upliftin' isn't it? *(Laughs)*
Upliftin', get it?
Where are you off to now?

ERIN: The beach. Can I get to the beach near here?

LINDA: Thornwick Bay, other side of the café. Take care, it's really steep.

ERIN: Thanks.

Wind band: scraping, sliding music with something of a dance feel.

ERIN: Scraping... and sliding.

Grazing my knee!

Down to the sands.

Down to the sea.

SCENE 4

We see two 'tombstoners' and a girlfriend at Thornwick Bay. Their spoken words are rhythmic. The two boys are preparing to jump. The girl is casually sunbathing.

SEAN: I'm on top of the world.

Cattee! Cattee!

CATTEE: Do you have any idea how high up you are?

SEAN: I can't hear you. I'm too high up!

CATTEE: This is so dangerous. Please get down.

NINER: Live a little.

CATTEE: I am living. I'd like to stay that way.

SEAN: Thornwick Bay: jumpin' off White Rock.

This is the bees' knees, doggg!

NINER: This is the cat's miaow!

The boys woof, miaow and whoop.

CATTEE: You two! You are so mad!

SEAN: Jumpin' from on high to feel we exist
with acrobatic flips like a gold medallist.

NINER: I can feel the words comin' –
We are the tombstonin' lyricists
scorin' a ten from the panellists.

SEAN: Yeah man!

NINER & SEAN: Jumpin' from on high to feel we exist
with acrobatic flips like a gold medallist.

(NINER & SEAN:)	We are the tombstonin' lyricists scorin' a ten from the panellist.
NINER:	This is the abyss!
SEAN:	This is the big drop!
NINER:	You gonna belly flop again, Sean?
SEAN:	No way. You are!

Mock fight.

CATTEE:	You're gonna get hurt, Sean. Sooner or later you're gonna get really hurt. Wish you cared enough about me to stop.
SEAN:	You know I care about you babe but a tombstoner's gotta do what a tombstoner's gotta do.
NINER:	We scramble on the rocks an' we relax in the bay but it's leapin' from a ledge that makes our day.
SEAN:	High velocity!
NINER:	Spiritual philosophy!
SEAN:	Seein' this view, it's like astronomy.
NINER:	We ain't thinkin' about the economy.

They whoop. They see ERIN *on the beach and nudge each other.*

SEAN:	Hey! Hey, blackalicious!
CATTEE:	I can't believe you just said that. You are so rude!
NINER:	Come on up, babe. You know you want to tombstone.
NINER & SEAN:	Tombsto-own! Tombsto-own! Tombsto-own! Tombsto-own!
CATTEE:	Don't mind them. They've only just learnt to walk on two legs.
	And they like trying to kill themselves.
ERIN:	What's 'tombstone'?
CATTEE:	Jumping from up high... into the sea. It's kinda stupid.
ERIN:	I'd love to jump into the sea.
(Sings)	'Jump if you jumpin!!' 'Jump if you jumpin!!'
NINER & SEAN:	Tombsto-own! Tombsto-own! Tombsto-own! Tombsto-own!

They repeat 'Tombstone' softly under ERIN'S *words until* 'Down, down, down'.

ERIN:
(*Singing to herself*)

Are they my bad angels?

Tempting me into the wilderness.

They are my bad angels.

I'll sink down down... down! Down, down, down.

We do not see IRENE *but we hear her words:*

IRENE:
(*Spoken*)

Don't do it, get through it.

Women get through it.

We are astonishingly brave girls.

ERIN: Promise me.

Pause.

I promised.

Me mum said   Me mum said

I should never break a promise.

Me mum...

She puts her hands together and shuts her eyes.

Help me keep her alive. Help me...

(ERIN:) *She walks slowly and meditatively along the cliff path.*

Can I get through it? I promised.

So why do I feel so alone?   So alone.

SCENE 5

Walk music. ERIN *arrives at 'Cancer Corner', just beyond the North Landing, below Marine Village. Images of Joe Caruso's joke boards.* VI, *a woman in her early seventies, is looking at the boards and laughing to herself.*

CHOIR: 'Laugh and live longer.'

VI: Oooh that's a good one:

CHOIR: 'It's not the stork in the morning that brings you —

VI: it's the lark at night.'

CHOIR: 'Laugh and live longer.'

VI *laughs and looks at* ERIN.

VI: You're not laughing, love.

  This is Joe Caruso's corner —
  Joe's laughing corner.

VI & CHOIR: Old Joe lives just there, with his gnomes.
  Gnome sweet home!

VI *laughs*.

VI: Joe's a magic man, an entertainer,
a Cancer Research campaigner.
Joe paints these jokes: you laugh, live longer.

VI & CHOIR: So put a penny or three in his container!

You get all sorts of folks
laughing at Joe's painted jokes
and if you're not a total spanner
you'll leave a donation for a scanner.

VI: Ooh, they call me rhyming Vi
from Haworth-on-High.

She laughs.

You're so sad, love, so sad.
You're so sad, love, so sad.

ERIN: My mum   she's ill   she's very ill

she could be dying.

Mum cared for my little girl
while I did my degree.
Now mum's so weak
she hardly speaks
and no-one's helping me,
no-one's helping me.

VI: I lost my little granddaughter… to cancer.

So I come to Joe's laughing corner.

(VI:)　　　　　And I do the Angel Cards.

　　　　　　　Messages from my angels.

　　　　　　　They help me get through it.

　　　　　　　She takes a pack from her pocket, closes her eyes, concentrates for ten seconds and then takes a card from the pack.

(Spoken)　　　Your angel for today is... Angel Caressa –

(Sung)　　　　'You are at the end of a cycle of your life.
　　　　　　　Let your angels guide you to your next step.
　　　　　　　Happiness awaits you now.'

VI & ERIN:　　 'Happiness awaits you now.'

VI:　　　　　　You've turned a corner, love,
　　　　　　　Joe Caruso's laughing corner.

ERIN:　　　　　It's just a card. There are no angels.

VI:　　　　　　Take it love. It's a gift from Vi.

ERIN *takes the card.*

VI:　　　　　　Remember, you've turned a corner.

ERIN *continues walking.*

ERIN:　　　　　I've turned a corner, my laughing corner!

　　　　　　　Oh we are astonishingly brave girls.

(ERIN:)	*She laughs.*
	'Happiness is waiting for me.'
	Those peregrines... they... guide me.
(Spoken)	A sign for... South Landing. South Landing!
	That's the beach! That's our beach!
	I'll find our beach, swim at our beach.

SCENE 6

Walk music. ERIN *continues walking, arriving at the fields on the way to South Landing.*

FARM BIRDS: *(Sung)*	Legs of twig and eyes of seeds, beaks of flint and wings of reeds.
ERIN:	This field... is full of birds.
ERIN:	I can't see them but I can hear them.
FARM BIRDS:	Legs of twig and eyes of seeds, beaks of flint and wings of reeds.
	Hid among the grasses there our hidden voices haunt the air. You can see us if you hush: skylark, warbler, thrush.
	We're woodcocks in the treetops who scatter if you sneeze.

(FARM BIRDS:) We're buntings on the fence posts
who sound like jangling keys.

Hid among the grasses there
our hidden voices haunt the air.
You may see us if you hush:
skylark, warbler, thrush.

ERIN *continues walking along the path, in a state of gathering excitement.*

SCENE 7

She picks up a feather and blows it into the air. Then she puts her arms out and 'flies' along the path, coming to a sudden stop as she sees the sculpture of the Flamborough Longsword Dance Lock.

ERIN:
(Spoken) It's a star, a kind of star.

An eight-pointed star... of... swords...

on a corner.

She laughs.

A laughing corner! It's a sign!

My angels have sent a sign.

She laughs.

I'll shimmy through it, get through it.

(ERIN:)   I'll start my new life.

She crawls through the star and looks down. As she crawls, the other two soloists sing:

SOLOISTS:
(Sung)   This Flamborough star against the sky
brings hope to life as fears die.
Pass through our star to reach the sky
where hope's the bird that's flying high.

ERIN: Down there, our beach,

our lovely rocky beach

...with rock pools!

SCENE 8

Accelerated walk music as ERIN *makes her way quickly down to South Landing.*

ERIN:
(Sung)   Pebbles under my feet.

Shingle under my feet.

I'll put my fingers in the sea.

Oooooh... it's freezing, it's freezing
but I am the astonishingly brave girl.

She takes her clothes off, stripping down to pants and shirt.

(ERIN:)
(*Spoken*)   I'm doing this for you, mum!

I'm doing this for you, Shaneka!

We're going to get through it.

I'll swim all our troubles away.

She runs into the sea and screams.

ERIN
& SOLOISTS: 'Five little ducks went swimming one day
(*Sung*)   Over the hill and far away.
              Mother duck said "Quack, quack, quack, quack"
              But only four little ducks came back!'

ERIN *hums the song to herself, breathlessly.*

ERIN: I feel like I could swim for ever... for ever and ever.

Sudden loud music, which gets louder. ERIN *is pulled down by the current.*

(*Spoken*)   Help! Help!

The SOLOISTS *repeatedly sing:*   The white darkness   the bright darkness   *beginning very softly and rising to a crescendo before fading away as* ERIN *and* ILONA *reach the safety of the shore in the following scene.*

ERIN:
(*Sung*)   I'm being pulled down.

(ERIN:)　　　so far down.

　　　　　　　Down, down, down.

ACT 3

SCENE 1

In the sea, off South Landing.

ILONA, *in a wetsuit, is struggling to support* ERIN, *who is panicking.*

Duet: ILONA's *and* ERIN's *lines overlap. They repeat sounds, words and lines.*

ERIN:
(Sung)　　　I want my mum!

　　　　　　　I want my little girl!

ILONA:
(Spoken)　　It's alright.　I've got you.

　　　　　　　Everything will be alright.

　　　　　　　Nearly there. Nearly there.

　　　　　　　Almost there.　Made it!

ILONA *holds* ERIN *until she revives a little.*

ERIN:
(Sung)　　　I felt like a feather... and then a stone,

(ERIN:)   a heavy stone.

ILONA *helps* ERIN *up, holding on to her.*

I'm so cold   so very cold!

You are... Ilona... from the cliffs.

ILONA: I must be your guardian angel.

You're shivering, like an egg.

ILONA *runs off, to get warm clothes from her bag for* ERIN. *We hear* IRENE *singing faintly, the first verse of Noel Coward's 'I'll see you again'.*

ERIN:
(Spoken)   I'm soooo cold, so very cold.

Pause.

Spitfire Irene?

IRENE'S *singing stops.* ILONA *returns.*

ILONA: Let's get you warm. Let me dry you.

ILONA *dries* ERIN, *who puts the clothes on.*

ERIN:
(Sung)   What are you doing here?

ILONA: This is the 'Flamborough Front'.

The best reef in England.

(ILONA:)   The rainforest of the sea.

We hear IRENE *singing faintly, but stronger than before, underneath* ILONA's *words.*

>Diving is like... birdwatching, but under the sea.
>
>Starfish, jellyfish, butterfish, sea urchins, anemones...
>
>maybe a porpoise.

SCENE 2

The beach below South Landing Great Scars.

IRENE: It's my astonishingly brave girl!

>You look cold. You need to get warm.
>
>Get warm by moving.   Like this.

She does a vigorous, slow and repetitive Tai Chi warm-up exercise. Then all three of them do the exercise, for about 50 seconds.

>I'm flying!   I'm flying!

They laugh. All the seabirds enter.

(Spoken)   Now we'll get warm by breathing,
             deep breathing.

She demonstrates a Tai Chi breathing exercise, in which the arms – as part of the exercise – spread out like wings at shoulder height.

> In through your nose
> Out through your mouth.
>
> In through your nose
> Out through your mouth.

ERIN *and* ILONA *join in and continue the exercise for about a minute and a half.*

ERIN: I'm really flying.

ILONA: And I'm sweating!

They laugh.

ERIN: I'm so happy.

> *Pause.*
>
> I must tell my mum... this is our beach.
>
> Oh my phone...

ILONA *takes a mobile phone out of an inside pocket in her bag.*

ILONA: Here.

ERIN *dials the number.*

ERIN: Hello? Hello mum, it's me, Erin.

(ERIN:) Yes, yes, I'm fine.

I'm at the beach, our beach...

Pause.

(Sung) Listen to the birds.   Listen to the birds.

She holds the phone up in the air. The seabirds continue to dance and then slowly sink down but still make precise movements with their hands.

Trio: the three voices overlap, but allowing space for us to hear each individual. Each of the three characters has a distinctive dance.

ERIN: I am a bird...

I am the astonishingly brave girl.

I'm flying, I'm flying.

ILONA: Look.   Listen.

This is our Serengeti.

This is our life on earth.

IRENE: I'm ninety now, ninety!

But woolly sleeves hide hidden wings

and deep inside a bird still sings.

As ERIN dances, ILONA and IRENE slowly leave. ERIN hugs herself as she sings. ILONA and IRENE repeat 'Hope is the thing with feathers' underneath ERIN's words.

ERIN: Now I am a grown-up girl
who's dancing by the sea.
I know I'll cope,
I'll get some help
for my precious family,
my precious family.

I know my mum will be so brave
and I'll get my degree.
I spread my wings
but I'll find time
for just my mum and me,
just my mum and me.

Some day I'll take my little girl
to a caravan by the sea.
There'll be rock-pool days
with sand and spades
and sometimes chips for tea,
sometimes chips for tea.

She slowly spins off. The dancers bring in puppet seabirds on long poles and fly them high in the air. Silence. The dancers leave slowly.

Our first image – a girl flies at Bempton Cliffs. (HS)

Wingbeats Photographers:

MJ	Malcolm Johnson	HS	Holly Strickson
TB	Tony Bartholomew	AS	Adam Strickson
SR	Steve Race	MS	Mark Smales

LightWeight with image of dancer on South Landing beach. (MS)

Dance workshop with East Riding Youth Dance, with spectator, at Bempton Cliffs. (AS)

Jane, our costume designer. (AS)

Balbir, our choreographer, flies a bird. (AS)

Flight Paths staging at The Spa. (MJ)

Bridlington Community Chorus. (MJ)

Gannet. (SR)

Erin and Ilona at Bempton Cliffs. (MJ)

Erin sings about her difficult life in Leeds. (MJ)

Our lithe and shining peregrines. (MJ)

The farm birds. (MJ)

Spitfire Irene. (MJ)

Linda and the puffin band. (MJ)

Erin meets Vi at 'Cancer Corner', Flamborough. (MJ)

Sword lock sculpture, above South Landing. (AS)

Erin at the sword lock sculpture. (MJ)

Ilona rescues Erin from the sea. (MJ)

Irene leads the Tai Chi. (MJ)

Natalie Raybould with the bust of Amy at Sewerby Hall. (TB)

Natalie flies at Sewerby Hall. (TB)

Adam and Jonathan rehearse the company. (MJ)

The ensemble. (MJ)

The fisher girls prepare. (MJ)

The sword dance lock. (MJ)

Paula with Amy's pigskin bag. (MJ)

Amy remembers flying. (MJ)

Amy and Jim's duet – 'Dual Control'. (MJ)

Amy and Jim after the crash. (MJ)

The girls prepare for the midwinter's eve bonfire. (MJ)

Paula sings about her useless boyfriend. (MJ)

Amy flies solo. (MJ)

AMY'S

LAST

DIVE

2012

Introduction

The background

Amy Johnson, the girl from Hull, paved the way for women today. She flew around the world, took huge risks and made history. In 1958, the 'Amy Johnson Collection' of souvenirs was presented by her father to Sewerby Hall, Bridlington. This provided the initial inspiration for *Amy's Last Dive*, especially her monogrammed pigskin bag which survived her final fatal crash.

On 5 January 1941, Amy was a member of the Aircraft Transport Auxiliary (ATA), ferrying all types of planes around the UK for the male pilots to take into the war of the skies. While flying from Blackpool to RAF Kidlington near Oxford, she went off course in poor weather. She drowned after bailing out into the Thames Estuary. Although she was seen alive in the water, the rescue attempt failed and her body was never recovered. The incident also led to the death of her would-be rescuer, Lieutenant Commander Walter Fletcher. There is still some mystery about the accident, and the exact reason for the flight is sometimes rumoured to be a government secret.

Throughout her short, action-packed life, Amy had tremendous physical energy. She vigorously expressed her attitude to the world through hockey, rambling, running, dancing, swimming, loving, aeronautical mechanics and – above all – flying. She was courageously physical. In the early 1930s, schoolgirls all over Britain put their arms out and ran around the playgrounds 'doing an Amy'. Our challenge in *Amy's Last Dive* was to re-enact this exuberant energy as 'a flight on the ground', communicating something of Amy's restless spirit and the great challenges she faced, both physically and in her dogged pursuit of an unusual career in the face of much opposition. *Amy's Last Dive* explores what it would be like for a young woman today to meet this challenging role model, and the place of love and solo flight in Amy's life.

The plot

We begin in 1934 when Amy Johnson's fame was at its height, four years after her solo flight to Australia. In Flamborough, on Yorkshire's East Coast, a group of young women, the Fisher Girls Dance Troupe, are preparing for their performance of the village's famous longsword dance at Leeds Town Hall. They talk about their heroine 'Amy, wonderful Amy' and their trip to the big city. Amy's ghost rises up in the final lock, or 'star', of the dance and the chorus sing about her last moments in the snow above the sea.

We are then transported to midwinter's eve, 2010. Paula, a young woman from a Thames estuary town, is jogging along the beach. She finds a pigskin bag. Out of the fog, a weird, shivering figure emerges and asks for the bag, saying it contains her maps and charts. Paula says that if she promises to tell her who she is, she will return the bag after fetching a hot drink and a blanket.

Amy reflects on 'who she is'. We hear muffled groans from the bottom of an old rowing boat. A bandaged figure slowly rises: it is Jim Mollison, Amy's husband, looking as he did in hospital after they crashed near Connecticut on their dual flight across the Atlantic in 1933. Amy and Jim, the 'Flying Sweethearts', play out this flight and their tempestuous relationship, using the boat as their plane. They crash, thanks to Jim's insistence on a final push to New York without sufficient fuel. Amy resolves to 'fly solo forever', prefiguring their divorce.

In an interlude, also set on midwinter's eve 2010, a group of young people arrive to set up a bonfire on the beach. They reflect on their fears and dreams for the future. By implication, they are responding to Amy's courageous example.

Paula returns and Amy reveals her identity. Paula recalls hearing about Amy Johnson at junior school. She gives her the pigskin bag. Amy celebrates the real love of her life, 'Jason', the Gypsy Moth in which she flew to Australia. Her ghost disappears into the fog, leaving Paula with a renewed sense of purpose for her own future.

The structure

The opera loosely follows the structure of a fourteenth-century Japanese Noh play, in which it is typical for someone in the present to meet a ghost who recounts the highly charged emotional story of their life on earth. In the Noh play *Hagoromo* (The Feather Mantle) by Zeami, a spirit of the sky falls to earth and leaves her cloak, without which she cannot fly, on the bough of a tree. A priest finds the cloak and refuses to give it back until the spirit has told him her story through a dance. Similarly, Amy cannot fly until Paula returns the pigskin bag full of the necessary maps and charts.

Noh plays can be divided into JO, HA and KYU. JO-HA-KYU is a dynamic and continuous process, like the growing of a flower from seed to bloom. It may be translated as PRELUDE–BREAKING–RAPID. In *Amy's Last Dive*, JO is the appearance of the ghost, HA is Amy and Jim's love duet and transatlantic flight and KYU Amy's hymn to the thrills of solo flight. Each part of JO-HA-KYU can be divided again in the same fashion. The structure I have developed for the opera reflects this, offering a rising and falling repetitive pattern of action that evolves and flows onwards, much like Amy's life.

The tradition of the Noh theatre is unbroken from the fourteenth century to the present. It contains elements which we might consider more appropriate to conventional ballet or opera than to a contemporary stage play: elaborate sculptural costumes, continuous music, intense spiritual dances, a mystery and a clear morality shown through the action – all of equal dramatic significance to the words that are recited in a heightened, 'unnatural' manner. A Noh play has been described as 'a lyrico-dramatic tone-poem in which the text has a function somewhat similar to that of the libretto in a Wagner or Debussy opera'. {The Japanese Classics Translation Committee (1955), *The Noh Drama*, Tokyo and Vermont: Charles E. Tuttle} The aesthetics of the total theatre that is the Japanese Noh has been a vital influence on my composition of libretti for contemporary opera.

The transformation object

The central feature of the production is an old wooden fishing boat. During the prelude this lies on its side and the audience may well not identify it as a boat. In a pile of beach detritus nearby, the remains of an aeroplane wing are hidden. When the fisher girls of Flamborough arrive for the prelude the boat is revealed; it could be a fishing boat on the North Bay beach in 1934 or today. Jim Mollison hides in the boat as if he is a mummy in an Egyptian tomb. The boat becomes Jim and Amy's hospital bed in New York. The white roses from the Roosevelts are a couple of pieces of dry grass in a drink can. The boat then becomes *Seafarer*, the plane in which Amy and Jim excitingly cross the Atlantic. Jim doesn't wear a flying helmet but a colander found on the beach. The steering mechanism is a piece of driftwood. When the plane crashes, Amy and Jim are thrown out of the boat onto the beach, which has become the swamp at the end of the runway in Connecticut. During the interlude, the boat is turned on its end, driftwood is piled against it and the plane wing is placed on top; it has become a midwinter solstice bonfire. Finally, in the KYU section, Amy stands on top of the boat and flies to Australia. It is now the cockpit of Jason, her plane, and a sacrificial fire on which she will 'burn', like Joan of Arc. At the conclusion of the opera, she disappears and the boat is a boat once again.

In much of my work, I have used objects in a similar way, influenced by a theatre exercise, the Noh's intensification of a single image and Peter Brook's practice. When I was studying Japanese theatre during my first degree at Dartington College of Arts, Peter Hulton introduced an exercise in which we had to begin moving one arm. We were not supposed to think but to allow the movement to change gradually and almost imperceptibly, not imposing a narrative but 'going with the flow'. This nurtured a kind of spontaneous play in which there was no stop and start. There was no beginning, middle and end and no attempt to define the image from one transformation to another. To borrow from the language of phenomenology, the image was always in a state of becoming. Behind this exercise, the Noh aesthetic of JO-HA-KYU is present and the idea of theatre as play. The action of all Noh plays clusters around a single image, the burial mound of *Sumidagawa* or the feather mantle of *Hagoromo*, just as the action of Amy depends on a wooden boat. But this boat is not a decorative precious object as in the Noh but a kind of giant toy for adult actors.

In Peter Brook's work and particularly in his production of

Jarry's *Ubu* (Théâtre des Bouffes du Nord, 1977) objects can become anything in front of our eyes just as actors can become anyone or anything. The only set for Ubu was a couple of cable drums and some bricks, which were transformed into whatever was required by the action. Piled on top of each other the cable drums became a throne and when they were rolled along they became a chariot. The bricks became the plates and the food at the Ubus' dinner party. This approach came out of years of play with his actors, using children's games to explore status and power relationships. Actors should always, in a way, remain as a gang of imaginative children. The transformational power of theatre is demonstrated by the imaginative play demonstrated both in rehearsal and before the audience. The play as play is what makes Kneehigh such a joyously inventive company; it is a unique and precious gift found in the experience of live, storytelling theatre.

Extracts from 'Amy's Last Dive: Diary of an Opera': a blog by Cheryl Frances-Hoad

Cheryl's witty and illuminating blog documents the composition of *Amy's Last Dive*. She wrote: 'This is my first full-length opera and I thought it might be fun to document the process of creating it, from the beginning to the hopefully decidedly un-bitter end.'

January 2012

Why Amy Johnson?

The simple answer to this is that Adam Strickson asked me to be involved in this opera, and had already come up with the basic subject matter and plot. Adam won an award from imove, part of the Yorkshire cultural programme for London 2012, for a large-scale project called Wingbeats, which includes this opera, another opera which has already been performed called *Flight Paths,* with music by Steve Kilpatrick, and many other wonderful arts projects and events. Although I didn't really know anything about Amy Johnson at all when Adam asked me to be involved, I quickly realised after talking with him that this was a wonderful subject for an opera and everything about Amy appealed to me, both personally and artistically.

In preparation for writing the libretto, Adam had read a fantastic biography of Amy by Midge Gillies. It was great to go through this book and pick out all the things that interested me about Amy, and tell Adam about them. In this way, even though the original idea had not been mine, I felt

I was able to put a great deal of input into the content of the opera and very soon felt that it was 'our' opera rather than just Adam's. As it happened though, Adam had already independently written a short summary of what interested him, and it almost exactly matched what I'd noted down. So that was a good sign!

In the summer, I went up to Bridlington to see the premiere of *Flight Paths*. I was able to see the venue, and spent a few days in the town soaking up the atmosphere. On the Sunday I did a 20-mile walk along the coast, which actually gave me so many ideas for the opera! The scenery was amazing (despite the fact that at one point I got lost for about an hour in thick bramble and then slipped down a very muddy bank and got covered in mud...) and I can honestly say I've never enjoyed fish and chips as much as I did at the end of that walk before getting the train back to my B&B in Brid. Amy spent a lot of time in the area, and so things I had read about in the biography and only known cerebrally suddenly made proper sense. For instance, spending a whole day walking along the edge of the country, where land runs out and seeing the sea and the horizon really had a great effect on me, and is something I'm thinking about a lot now I've started writing the opera far out of sight of any coastline. The seemingly seamless merging of sea and sky in the far distance is something that I'm trying to portray in the harmony of the work, either by using very 'open-sounding' harmony, or by merging harmonic boundaries into each other. Just being able to see so far into the distance also made a great impression on me, and the horizon is a very important element of Amy's story in many ways – that sense of exploration, the urge to travel beyond what she could see, etc. I also learnt later that the way pilots learn to stay level in their planes is to continually keep their position in check with the horizon. There's something about this double function of the horizon, which coaxed Amy into undertaking dangerous adventures as well as keeping her safe and up in the air, that really fascinated me.

Anyway, I came back from Bridlington really excited about the opera, about Amy and about the performances, which at this point in time seemed so far in the future that they might never happen. This was all to change when I realised how much work I had to do, though! Suddenly that premiere seemed terrifyingly close...

Meeting the libretto...

So, by this time, I had a clear idea in my head about Amy's character, and I knew roughly what was going to happen in the opera. There was a lot I could do before I got the libretto (I spent many enjoyable hours listening to 30s big band music, which Amy would have frequently heard (and in fact Jack Hylton wrote a song about her called 'Amy, Wonderful Amy') thinking how I could get used to this 'research' malarkey...) but really the proper compositional planning could only be started once I got the words...

It's always quite nerve-wracking when you first meet a libretto. Even though I knew and loved Adam's poetry, and knew we had very similar ideas about the opera's 'story', there's always a tiny element of 'what if I hate it?!' panic when you first open the cover of any text that you know you'll be living with constantly for the next six months of your life. I quickly realised this fear was completely unfounded, however, and I absolutely loved what Adam had written. We met in a café in Huddersfield and Adam read through the text he had written (due to the opera's quick turnaround he gave me several scenes to begin work on, as he will finish the libretto whilst I am beginning to set scenes which he has already written). I left a cold and grey

Huddersfield full of excitement about opera, although by now the terror and reality of actually having to do some work was beginning to set in...

How to start?

I find starting a new composition *terrifying*. And the more I compose, the more terrifying it gets. Whether it's a short piano piece or a large-scale chamber work, I still devote much of my time and energy at the beginning of the compositional process to *not* starting. In fact one of the only times you will find my house in a tidy state is when I'm 'starting' a piece. So as the prospect of actually having to write something huge became a reality, I decided that by far the most sensible thing to do would be to block it all out and go and book a flight in a Gypsy Moth, the plane in which Amy flew to Australia during 1930. During this time I also read copious literature about blind flying (flying with only the instruments in the cockpit, necessary in low/zero visibility conditions), became an expert on thermal air currents and how to tell the different types from each other by examining the different cloud formations present, read a whole dissertation on David Beckham's accent, transcribed lots of big band music and five Lily Allen songs, and watched a fair amount of 1960s BBC newsreader clips and several *The Only Way is Essex* episodes on YouTube, ALL in the name of research. [...]

Unfortunately, when the day came to fly a Gypsy Moth, the wind conditions were too high, but my would-have-been instructor nevertheless took me out to see the plane in the hangar and let me climb inside. The most amazing thing about it was that you couldn't see in front of you because the cockpit came above your sight line, so in order to see ahead you had to stick your head out the side! This was quite easy when on the ground... but at 80mph in heavy rain things would be very different. [...]

Coincidentally I am the same height as Amy Johnson, a rather stunted 5 foot 4 inches, so I really could appreciate what it would have been like for her, stuck in that tiny cockpit for hour upon endless hour. This is something I'd not have really 'known' if I hadn't experienced it, and that sense of not seeing ahead of you will be constantly in my mind when I'm writing the music to the scene where Amy and her husband Jim Mollison cross the Atlantic together. During the crossing they had to really put their trust in the instruments in the cockpit's 'dashboard' (I'm sure you don't call it this but you know what I mean...) All those dials continually altering, and the skill in deducing the aircraft's position through reading their combined data, will really have an effect on the musical fabric at this point in the work. For instance, when the plane is tossed about like a car on a bumpy road on the air currents, the altimeter would be varying by small-to-large amounts at a frequent rate, whereas the compass would vary at a much more gradual, constant rate. The combination of these two types of movement, one erratic, one more constant, could be portrayed directly in the rhythm and melodic movement of, for instance, two of the instrumental parts. The way that all the dials come together to make some sort of sense, but are fairly useless individually, could affect the contrapuntal treatment of a particular passage (e.g. each part could be 'incomplete' itself, but add up to a coherent melody of texture when in combination with the whole ensemble) [...]

Why David Beckham/TOWIE and BBC newsreaders from the 60s, you ask? Well, each of the characters in the opera has a very specific accent (Paula, a girl living near the Thames estuary in 2010, has an estuary accent in my mind, whilst Jim Mollison spoke in very proper RP), and in order to really get under their skins, I wanted to be able to get as near to what would have been their voices into my ear in order to intuitively place these essentially melodic vocal inflections into the music. Again, it's not an exact copy I'm really after – this isn't a big-budget biopic where every gesture and vocal inflection of the lead role should be copied and perfectly reproduced, after all. But our voices are so much part of us, and convey such a great deal of our characters, that it's really important to me that I fully understand this before composing.

One specific example is Amy Johnson herself. I managed to find a ten-minute clip of her, which included quite a bit of footage of her speaking, on YouTube. Even before she had touched down on Australian soil, Amy had become one of the first ever celebrities, after being an unknown, underestimated pilot, who many people thought should be occupying herself with finding a husband and cooking his dinner, when she left Croydon airport at the beginning of her trip. One of the clips shows her being driven through the streets in an open-top car, with a man supporting her elbow while she waves (as she was so exhausted after her flight that she hardly had the strength hold her arm up, but the public appetite for her was such that she was given hardly any time at all to herself to recover). She was a girl from Hull who had been thrust into superstardom, but in the video clips her slight awkwardness (or perhaps just exhaustion) is very evident. She tends to speak a little too fast, with fairly frequent, awkward pauses where she struggles to think of things to say, and she has a tendency to place stresses on words which you wouldn't usually stress. Melodically her voice is a fairly high monotone, with the odd much higher note when she says something like, 'I'm having *such* a wonderful time.' This overemphasis on the word 'such' gives a sentence like this a kind of forced nature – a feeling of having to perform for the public and pretending to be oh-so-delighted to see everyone – which perfectly conveys her situation at the time.

Amy said she felt more at home in the air, so one of my ideas was to let her sing completely fluidly and un-stintedly when she was either flying or talking about flying, which would contrast with parts of the opera where she was talking about other aspects of her fame, which she was uncomfortable with, whereupon some of the vocal traits noted above might come to influence the content of the vocal line. It's amazing how an awareness of this has really helped me define Amy's character and give her an identity in the actual musical material of the opera. And exactly the same goes for Paula with her estuary accent, and Jim with his plummy Queen's English.

Oh, more about Lily Allen in a later post...

On being very glad about living in a detached house in the middle of nowhere...

I recently moved to a little house in the middle of nowhere (there is one bus a week, so if using public transport you can either get out for two hours, or a week and two hours...) and decided to experiment with completely cutting myself off from the outside world. I find composing ridiculously difficult, even though I can't imagine ever doing anything else for the rest of my life, and the more I do of it, the more difficult I find it [...]

I've been setting a rather steamy (and at times hilarious) love scene between Amy and Jim. As I'm sure every pioneering aviating couple do, they choose to seduce themselves in the language of aircraft parts...

So, most of today has been taken up with trying to first vocalise, work out the rough notes of, and then notate different ways of saying 'Oh Jim' and 'Oh Johnnie' (Jim Mollison's nickname for Amy Johnson) in a variety of sexually provocative ways that would be more than at home in a particularly saucy scene in a *Carry On* movie. I think the postman may think I'm a total nutcase. But let's just say there are lots of different ways to say/sing these words, and some of them contain intervals as large as a 10th...

I'm setting this entire number as a somewhat deranged 30s music hall number, with instrumental, improvisational-like interludes which gradually get more and more overexcited and harmonically unhinged as Amy and Jim find more and more innuendo-laden airplane parts to use as euphemisms. I have been having the time of my life doing this and am wondering whether I'm wasted in the classical world and had better move into B-movie soundtrack writing...

Anyway, more about the music that is currently inspiring the opera another day, I think. There is still plenty of innuendo-laden text to set... 'Yes, yes, yes you are my Tiger!' (as in Tiger Moth...)

Finding Paula

In the last week I've been setting a monologue by Paula, one of the three main characters in the opera. Without wanting to spoil the plot, I think it's safe to say that there are several different time periods within the opera – that of the modern day, and those of the time when Amy was still alive.

Near the beginning of the opera we see Paula jogging along by the Thames estuary, thinking about how she wants to improve her life ('I will spend less time on Facebook': how I identify with that line of the libretto...!)

Some parts of the text immediately suggest the way that they should be set, but with Paula's monologue this was not the case: I found her character quite hard to pinpoint and got stuck for quite a while on this section. As Paula and Amy are in very different places in their life, and are/were living in very different times and cultures, I wanted to find some musical way to represent this difference. Also, I had the feeling that Paula, although she has the potential to really 'live' life, is trapped in a rather superficial existence, even though (whether she currently realises it not) she is searching for some kind of deeper meaning to life. But in the end, after all the sitting at the piano trying to think profound thoughts about musical character representation, well, the idea of how to set this passage came to me while I was jogging...

I've decided to set this song in a quasi pop-song format, with intros, bridges, choruses and verses. Paula repeats mantras to herself about how she will improve her life and herself, and I could imagine her saying these things repeatedly and increasingly confidently on her jog, as she gets buoyed up by her endorphin-boosting run. Also, in harmonic terms, I wanted to start with something fairly straight, almost banal, and gradually add more and more harmonic colour as the song progressed, as Paula becomes more confident about enriching her existence and we see her potential to do so.

So, in the name of research again, I decided to crack open a bottle of wine and spend the evening plugged into my iPod, playing along to Lily Allen songs all night. It was surprisingly enjoyable.

To be honest I didn't think I'd gain a great deal from harmonic analysis of Lily Allen songs but I actually learnt quite a lot that I tried to musically internalise and then reproduce in my own musical improvisations later on that evening and the following day. (I should say, I spent about eight hours doing all this, before I even thought about setting any words. I suppose if I do something I decide to do it quite a lot...) For instance, the harmony in many of her songs is very repetitive, but (I certainly find that) one can easily get lost in the music and not realise quite how repetitive the music actually is: rather than getting bored you get lulled into a groove etc. (but I am the kind of person who will listen to one song repeatedly for weeks, so maybe this is just me). I think one of the reasons behind this might be a scarcity of dominant 7th chords at the end of phrases or four-bar riffs, so there's a lack of the question-and-answer-type tension you get in classical music. One notable exception to this is at the end of the bridge before a return to a chorus, for example, when that sense of return to something is desired. Also, and this I know is stating the obvious, but the chords are usually very simple. Adding any blue notes (which is basically all I do with my harmony) made my 'pop song' sound too jazzy, and I didn't want that, but using only major and minor harmonies just sounded too derivative. In the end I decided to use fairly conventional harmony (major or minor chords with usually only one or two, non-bluesy notes added) in unusual progression, and this seemed to do the job of referencing the music that Paula would probably be listening to at the same time as (hopefully) making the music sound my own.

Do Amy, Jim and Paula know they are in an opera?

One thing that's gradually been dawning on me to think about in the last few weeks is whether my characters actually know they are in an opera or not. And I've decided the answer is both; or at least, sometimes they are more aware of the theatricality of their performances than at other times. Or perhaps it's always ambiguous, I'm not sure. I got to thinking about this when I was writing Amy and Jim's seduction duet. Are they simply going over the top in a sort of over-the-top, raunchy, *Carry On* way that I have the feeling might have floated Jim Mollison's boat, or are they deliberately camping it up for the audience or simply for their own theatrical enjoyment? It's probably a bit of all three.

In Paula's jogging scene, is she being herself, talking to herself, or perhaps getting the more motivated part of herself to talk to the lazy Paula; is she just proclaiming these promises to the Thames estuary, or to us in the audience?

I'm not really sure but I'm really enjoying playing around between the boundaries of these viewpoints. That last sentence makes me sound rather more cerebral than I actually am. To be honest I try not to think about this stuff too much and just spend the day singing and playing the piano, trying to create the most expressive and characterful phrases that I can. I have a slight fear that if I think too much my brain will fall out and it will all stop working, and I'll suddenly be unable to write anything...

February 2012

Jim Mollison: a bally good explorer, even if he was a drunken womaniser...

Recently I've been setting more music for Jim Mollison. Until this point all I'd really written was his part in the aviation-term seduction duet, where for the most part he is indulging in innuendo-laden banter, and, well, this certainly only represents one side of his character...

Like Amy, he would often dress up to the nines for aviation. In this I totally approve... I, erm, had my premiere dress organised for this opera before I'd written a note, and currently own three aviation-themed brooches, and probably will own more in due course (there are more than three performances of this opera, don't you know...) The dress was 90% off in the Harvey Nics sale so was actually a compulsory buy. Fact.

Anyway, I digress. Jim's nickname was 'Brandy Mollison', as he had a habit of taking flasks of brandy and other beverages with him in the cockpit, imbibing copious amounts on his record-breaking flights. And by all accounts he was a terrible womaniser...

Amy refused to believe that the marriage couldn't be rescued until she found Jim drunk in a hotel room with a woman she didn't recognise...

So, it's pretty apparent that Jim wasn't exactly ideal husband material and all that, being as he was an arrogant, womanising, heavy-drinking man who resented Amy's greater fame.

However, he was still a bloody good pilot who undertook some amazing, life-threatening, courageous journeys, and in the opera I really want to portray a little of this. This opera is very much about Amy, and Jim's function is largely to help tell Amy's story, but I still didn't want to reduce him to a caricature, as if nothing else, he wouldn't be that attractive and surely one has to be moderately-to-exceedingly attractive in at least one way to be a successful womaniser (God, I have the feeling this might be a hideously un-PC thing to say, but you know what I mean). Simply put, I wanted to be able to rather fancy Jim's character in the opera, or at least see what Amy saw in him at points, rather than roll my eyes at what an up-himself berk he was.

Jim has the line 'Just you and me and the sky and the sea' several times in the Atlantic crossing scene. I really like the mixture of naivety, wonder, courage, childishness and affection in this line (as amongst other things he's obviously happy that Amy is with him). There's a kind of faux charm about the line that is very simplistic, but when you think about it, it sums up a variety of emotions from joy and freedom to terror (Amy hated flying over water). I wanted to set these lines in a way that would give us a glimpse into Jim's pioneering spirit, and the fact that (at first, anyway)

Amy and Jim were excellent, professional flying companions.

Anyway, this is all well and good but I was completely stuck on this for a few days.

There were several reasons for this. Firstly, I've just been composing nonstop for several months now (I've written 35 minutes of music in less than six weeks, way over my usual output) and I feel I am something of a compositional corpse (just as well I have a week of not composing coming up, which I'm slightly terrified about in one way but I think a short, enforced break might be very good idea). Secondly, this was the last scene of the opera I had, as I hadn't had the final third of the libretto from Adam yet. The Atlantic crossing scene is humorous, and I love it, but it came directly after the seduction duet, which was also humorous. I was a bit worried by the fact that there wasn't enough serious stuff in the opera to balance things out, put simply. But this was completely solved when I saw the final third of the opera, which is a wonderfully passionate, expansive aria for Amy. This reassured me that I could follow my instincts on how to set the Atlantic crossing, as there would be music of greater depth to provide contrast and balance in the remaining part of the opera.

So, that was that aspect of the problem solved. But I still didn't really know how to set it, until David Attenborough came to my rescue.

(Comment from Adam:) The apparently banal line 'Just you and me and the sky and the sea' sums up some of the things I've learnt about libretto-writing in the past couple of years. It does all sorts of things both in sound and content: a) It's rhythmic. b) It's easy to repeat and for the singer to put a different spin of subtext on the meaning each time it's repeated. c) It's actually more about Amy than Jim, who is singing – so this line's content is also her physical reaction

to a sort of provocation by Jim. D. It holds different layers of meaning if the listener wishes to find them – Amy hates the sea and is terrified of it; Amy and Jim have a difficult relationship and, in many ways, Amy would rather be flying solo than being 'you and me'; the act of flying over the Atlantic is extremely dangerous but Jim can reduce it to a song lyric. There's an echo of 'tea for two and two for tea', the kind of charming London romance that Amy and Jim began with. Sing something simple and there's so much going on – in this case perhaps more for the character who is not singing at this moment in the action.

Dancing across the Atlantic

Sometimes one just seems to have a stroke of luck – I suppose it's partly to do with being very open to suggestion when one is inspired (if that doesn't sound hideously affected). You know, those times when you walk past a billboard with some crappy advert on it that nevertheless triggers off something that gives you an idea, or when you turn on the radio to catch something totally fascinating that ends up becoming a new piece twelve months later. I was very glad to have used *Desert Island Discs* as my procrastinatory tool of choice that morning.

When David told us about his third disc, it became obvious: a waltz was like the perfect way to set the Atlantic crossing! I think I actually said 'aha!' in an embarrassingly declamatory fashion whilst throwing my arms up in the air at this point (another reason why I'm probably best off living alone at the moment).

Both Amy and Jim were the epitome of 1930s glamour. The idea of a plane as a bird somehow tied in – the grace of a bird and the grace of a dancer. The fact that they were working as a couple, swapping places in the cockpit (like whirling round on a dance floor). The outward elegance alongside the hidden sweat and muscle-ache of top-class dancing paralleled the elegance of the long-distance flight, Amy touching up her makeup and hair before she touched down having not slept for several days straight and on the verge of collapse. The ability of the waltz to be both slightly twee, naive and comic at the same time as passionate and expansive (something that I really went for during Jim's second statement of 'Just you and me and the sky and the sea.') The ability to 'off-kilter-ise' a waltz by occasionally inserting a 5/8 or 7/8 bar (lengthening or shortening the 3/4 bar by a quaver so that the second 'cha' of the 'umm-cha-cha' rhythm is either slightly too short or too long, so as to represent the plane being buffeted by the winds, being thrown off course etc. etc.).

I got very excited about this and wrote almost all of Jim's material for this scene that day. The waltz pattern also allowed me to clearly present sometimes quite complex harmony – I had in my ear harmony for both England (the start point) and New York (the intended end point) and wanted to play about with gradually moving from one type of harmony to the other (very simplified, England equated to pastoral E minors and F majors in my mind, whilst New York was full of sharp-9 chords and F sharp minor/major).

Amy comes to lunch

Despite the previous moan about just getting inspired and having to stop (which is basically how my work pattern generally seems to go) I was really excited about last Saturday when Natalie Raybould, who is going to sing Amy in the opera, came to visit and sing through what I'd written so far.

Basically, Natalie had completely got what I was wanting,

which is mostly down to the fact that she is totally fantastic, but hopefully also in part to the fact that I'd been successful in imbuing the music with as much character as I could. I always find it difficult knowing how much to put in the score when writing for voices – I tend to put in fewer instructions as a) the words suggest a lot of the emotion, and b) I'm not sure one can use so much of one's brain to think about dynamics when singing (and in this case acting too) as when playing. Not sure about this. Perhaps it's just because, in vocal music, due to the necessity of getting the words across as clearly as possible (which is very important to me for the vast majority of the time) there are actually less dynamic variations in the melodic lines.

Natalie understood the influences of the music, whilst still kindly saying that it had retained my own voice. I said to her that I was really pleased about this, as over the last few months I'd spent a lot of time trying to really internalise, and then forget, music as diverse as Jack Hylton's 30s dance music and Lily Allen. I think that's really quite important – to really get under the skin of a kind of music (if that's what inspires your music), really get the feel of it and understand how it works, and then try and forget as much as possible and compose your own music, which can't help being influenced by the music you've got to know so well in some way or other. Seems to work for me, anyway.

On Saturday, everything crystallized. I thought I'd tell you how.

On Saturday 25th February I got all the ideas for the Atlantic crossing. Days like this are great. I haven't known how to set this bit for a while, couldn't quite put my finger on it, but now, after weeks of putting it out of my mind and writing other bits instead, it finally all came together. Days like this are also great because one feels one does a tremendous amount of work with hardly any effort, which in my book is really the way it should always be but never is. Things click into place, things which were perplexing suddenly become obvious, and connections become apparent and tangible between things and other things that previously seemed totally unrelated.

As soon as everything came together I had to stop, as I had to go to a performance of a piano trio of mine the next day and now as I type am on my way up to Leeds to teach. But I thought I'd put down on paper all my thoughts about how I'm going to compose this section first, before I actually write it, and then, when I've finished it in a week or so, I'll tell you what I actually did.

The last section that I set involved Amy and Jim embarking on their joint Atlantic crossing. The part that I was worried about was the section directly after this – where they start to run out of fuel and then crash.

So, it's basically a section in two parts – they start off in England in the first part, run out of fuel over the USA and crash in the second. I wanted to represent the change of continents with a change in harmony – in simple terms from English pastoral to New York cool. So the first sections are based around E and F chords, moving in to F sharp majory/minory chords in the second (as they just 'fit', to me). The first bit is set to a sort of off-kilter waltz (see a few blogs back) and the second will be completely different – variable time signatures etc. with very likely a constant quaver motion running throughout.

Thinking about pacing, this is going to move rather fast, and the rhythm is going to be repetitive but with 'spluttering' breaks in it that will increase, due to the gradual failure of the engine (as it runs out of petrol). Harmony-wise, I spent an hour or so looking through Mark Levine's *Jazz Piano* book, as I wanted to find jazz-influenced harmony that would sound very 'urban': I think to Jim New York might be some kind of socialising Mecca. The chapter on upper-structure chords was what I was looking for, and in fact simply playing through the table of the nine upper-structure chords sounds really great on its own. In other parts of the opera the chords span a wide distance – sometimes in a five-note chord each interval may be more than an octave apart. In this section I am going to keep the top and bottom notes of the chord quite close together – probably under two octaves. This is partly just for variety, and partly because I want to use chord melodies, with all the parts playing in parallel motion, going up and down, mimicking the motion of the airplane as Amy continually urges Jim to get the nose higher and circle in order to lessen the impact of the crash. This will be more apparent if the chords are quite narrow in range as they will be able to go up and down over wide distances without going out of instrumental ranges. The vocal parts are going to be quite rapidly delivered – they are after all in increasing panic, so they may be quite recitative-like over the busy orchestral writing.

Well, I think that's as good a place as any to stop for now. I'd better get on with writing it...

March 2012

A Bigger Picture

So, this week I went with my mum to see David Hockney's *A Bigger Picture* exhibition.

The day off at the Royal Academy of the Arts did me the power of good, and I got a really good idea whilst in the exhibition! I think it's something to do with the fact that when you're in the middle of writing, everything seems pertinent or relevant. But as it happens many of the pictures in Hockney's exhibition are of the area that Amy would have flown over (he lives in Bridlington now and the majority of the exhibition was made up of paintings of the landscape in the surrounding area). One of the pictures was almost like an aerial view of the local landscape – probably from the viewpoint of higher ground but it could have easily been the view from a low-flying plane. This painted view of the fields from above, in vibrant colours, gave me an idea for the harmonic structure of the last section of the opera, which could be said to be a hymn to the glory of flying.

So, anyway, I'm thrilled about this, as I'm just about to begin this section, and feel newly inspired.

It got me thinking about perspective too – in the opera are we looking up at Amy and Jim flying? Are we in the plane with them looking down at the landscape, or are we viewing them from the air (as if in a separate plane)? Well, I realised when looking back at the music I've written that it's all three (at different times). I don't know if that's particularly pertinent, but it just struck me the other day... I suppose, however, that some of these things only occur to you after you've composed certain bits – and it's amazing how structurally things seem to fit into place, sometimes unconsciously. I've been surprised how well some of my themes fit together – when, in for instance a coda, the text harks back to previous material and I've tried to bring back the melodies associated with that material too. It's nice to have surprises like that.

April 2012

Piano score sent off!

Two days ago I sent the full piano score off to everybody, all the singers, the repetiteur, conductor etc. So the main bit of the opera (e.g. the bit just involving the professional singers) is done! I still have about 30 mins of music to write, but a lot of this will be fairly repetitive/background music underneath talking/acting etc. Still a massive amount of work to do but the psychological relief of sending my 132-page, 62-minute score off was quite massive!

With something of this length, even 'small' jobs take ages – working out the metronome marks for the whole work took 12 hours, putting in dynamics another full day, and instructions ('sadly' etc.) a good half-day. It was strange: I found putting words to the emotions I had created in the music very hard – it's almost as if I'd worked out so specifically exactly what I wanted in the notes that it had gone beyond words. Either that or I've been composing so much that I've lost the ability to use the English language properly. I expect it's a bit of both.

So, still a lot to do. Orchestrate, and write the material for the prologue and interlude, which, to be honest, is newish territory for me... I'll explain why in the next post.

The prologue and interlude

Adam and I met for what turned out to be about three hours, I think. I played the opera through to him rather badly, and then we discussed the prologue and interlude, which until then I hadn't thought about much, other than reading them through several times; although after I sent off the scores, I arranged the text out on the floor of the kitchen (I literally do spread all the pages out, in order to get a kind of spatial awareness of the structure of a section) and realised I had so many questions that it would be impossible to start until I'd spoken to Adam.

The questions are all about timings, basically – local young actors are going to be involved, and will be acting/speaking in these sections. Some parts will be partly improvised, perhaps, so obviously this has great implications for the music – most specifically, how long it should be. The other problem is that the stages in Leeds and Bridlington are very different sizes, so parts of these sections will vary in length in each location. This is fairly new territory for me – I have written a semi-improvised score for a radio play, but with this there was a great deal of silence. The music would come in for 30 seconds, say, and then fade out. I want the music of these two sections of the opera to be constant, so composing a kind of music which isn't totally inane (just endless repetitions) but that is also adjustable, not just in rehearsal but between performances in different venues, is going to be quite a challenge.

I'm sure once I get down to it things will become clear, and I already have quite specific ideas of the types of music that these sections will contain, but there's always this sense of slight terror before beginning a new big section of work. Anyhow, it was great to talk to Adam because we were able to time each section (which although not exact at least gives you an idea) and to clarify a great number of things. Adam said it was very useful for him too, as he'd been very busy with other projects, and had not really thought about these sections lately, but with rehearsals for the choir and for the actors approaching, it was becoming a necessity.

I will try to blog about this properly, but briefly: the prologue is set in 1934, and the interlude 2010. So, I'm basically planning to use influences from these two years in the music.

Everything fits into place

One of the things I've noticed when writing this opera is that things keep fitting magically into place. I think I'm so inside the music now that my unconscious must be doing some fairly cool stuff. Or maybe I'm just seeing increasingly pertinent connections between things, much as one does at the onset of some forms of mental illnesses. I don't mean this flippantly at all: the research that I sat in on at the Department of Psychiatry at Cambridge University when I was a Leverhulme Artist in Residence there a few years ago was looking at precisely this, and we had long discussions about the similarity of very early-onset psychosis to particular stages of the creative process.

Anyway, what really struck me was how easy it was to compose a bit at the end, where three voices overlap. Two of these phrases have been heard much earlier in the libretto, and I wanted to keep the original melodies that I had written.

However, it was Amy's text (that was relatively new, only having been heard in the preceding sections) that I decided to set first, and the idea for an accompaniment, which is a kind of irregular passacaglia (a fixed rhythm and a fixed choral melody, which have different lengths so it takes five quasi-repetitions for the two to get back in synch again), came fairly easily.

I thought I'd have to alter things a lot to fit the other melodies in, but as it happened they slotted in without any alteration in one part, and only the tiniest changes in another part. This struck me as quite amazing as none of the three melodies had been composed with the intention of fitting together (a bit of an oversight one might say, since they were layered over each other at the end of the libretto, but hey...)

The thing is, a lot of things like this have been happening since I've been writing this opera – little snippets of melodies from other sections magically work when layered over each other, motives from other voices slip into other vocal parts when characters are trying to influence each other, or taking on each other's characteristics, etc. etc. It's one of the real joys of composing for me – when you are so inside the music you are writing that these things just work without much effort on your part.

Writing an opera is very tiring, I find – just the long-haulness of it is psychologically draining, but the other side of it is that, having lived with the music for five months now, I know it better than I realised, and the ease with which some ideas have come to me has been quite wonderful.

May 2012

On being tormented by folk tunes

In the last few days I've been suffering from inadvertently-blurting-out-folk-songs syndrome. They are just so stuck in my head I'm wondering if they'll ever leave me. It was when I realised I'd been singing along with the beat of the car indicator that I realised it had got serious.

This is largely due to the fact that in the last few days I've spent most of my days with the folk tunes that sword dancers dance to. In the opera there are three one-minute sword-dance sections. I love this kind of work... I wanted to create interesting and quirky arrangements of the melodies, whilst still having them retain their character. I've managed to do all sorts of things – layer three folk tunes on top of each other, one of which works at a canon of a crochet etc., and then, amazingly, the main folk tune that I'm using fits really well over a chorus that I wrote months ago (before I'd listened to the folk tune). I guess my interpretation of 'fitting' is slightly more relaxed than a lot of people's, but I'm generally quite thrilled.

Panic

I am increasingly being overwhelmed by panic that I'm not going to be able to finish this opera. It's 381 pages and counting, and I've still got eight minutes of music to write. It will get done, but as the deadline approaches there is still such a ridiculous amount of work to do. I think I'm also quite scared of finishing it: living with something this big for seven months makes you intensely protective of your work, and the thought of anybody not thinking that 100% of it is utterly brilliant is quite hard to contemplate. That sounds very pretentious. I guess the thing is to just carry on...

Finished (kind of)

I put the last note in the opera this morning.

When I can bear to look at this computer screen again, perhaps tomorrow, I shall blog about it.

I still have to put all the dynamics in to the computer score, and there is still a lot of work to do, but, well, since the last post was entitled 'Panic' I thought I should do this short update.

But first there is sun to be soaked up and perhaps a glass of wine to be drunk.

June 2012

End of week two of rehearsals

Well, by some miracle I actually finished the opera, even though it involved quite a few 19-hour days, including one particularly horrible one when I realised that rehearsal marks didn't match up between the vocal and full scores. But it all worked out well in the end and seeing the published scores helped to convince me that it was actually done! Finishing something this big was quite a bizarre feeling and I felt without purpose for quite a few days. I always get that feeling but this time it was particularly pronounced!

Anyway, so almost immediately the rehearsals started (the singers had had their scores for a few months, as I wrote the community participation sections and did the orchestration last).

To be honest, when I finished the score, the last thing I wanted to think or hear about was Amy Johnson! But my enthusiasm has been totally revitalised by being in rehearsals. It's SO amazing to see people bring what was in my (and Adam's) head to life. Also amazing to see all the things other than the words and music – as I type this I'm watching the lighting being plotted, and over the last week, when I've been practising (I have to play the piano for the Friday performances) I've seen the set taking shape (designed by Hannah Sibai).

The instrumentalists are great, and everything is taking shape really quickly, in no small part down to Jonny Lo, the fabulous conductor working on this project. It's a wonderful feeling as a composer to feel that you don't really have to say anything in rehearsal because the conductor understands exactly what you are aiming at, and this is definitely the case with Jonny. I've learnt to be pessimistic at the beginning of orchestral rehearsals – no matter how good the musicians are (and they are very good!) the music always sounds a little muddy in the beginning stages – but then, as the musicians get to know each other and the music, and 'get' the music, as it were, then it's like a camera lens gradually focusing. You hear all the little details that were clear in your head, and that's when for me it gets really exciting!

Amy's Last Dive

A Story of Flight, Ambition and Courage

a Wingbeats performance, was commissioned by imove and formed part of the Cultural Olympiad in Yorkshire and Ludus Festival, Leeds.

It was premiered on the 28th June 2012 at the Workshop Theatre at the University of Leeds.

Four further performances took place at the Workshop Theatre on the 29th June and on the 6th July 2012 at The Spa, Bridlington.

WRITTEN AND DIRECTED BY Adam Strickson
COMPOSED BY Cheryl Frances-Hoad

MUSICAL DIRECTOR: Jonathan Lo
CHOIR LEADER: Emily Smith
DESIGNER: Hannah Sibai
DESIGN CONSULTANT: Becs Edwards
LIGHTING DESIGN: Paul Halgarth
STAGE MANAGER: James Thompson
CONSTRUCTION: Ian Lindley
PRODUCTION MANAGER & DRAMA WORKER: Rebecca Jenkins

WINGBEATS PROJECT DIRECTOR: Lara Goodband
WINGBEATS PRODUCER FOR IMOVE: Jenny Harris

Cast

AMY JOHNSON: Natalie Raybould
JIM MOLLISON: David Pisaro
PAULA: Rebecca Lea

Musicians

SAX/CLARINET: Robin Porter
FLUTES: Christian Fernqvist and Lindsey James
OBOE: Bea Hubble
VIOLIN: Hannah Padmore
VIOLA: Emily Pond
CELLO: Jessica Burroughs
DOUBLE BASS: Vanessa McWilliam
PERCUSSION: Enrico Bertelli
PIANO: Edward Caine/Cheryl Frances-Hoad (on film)

Bridlington Community Chorus

Sally Wilkinson, Ann Hatfield, Beverley Fieldhouse, Gill Andrews, June Clough, Maureen Gainey, Sheila Cadman, Sue Gollop, Tricia Holroyd, Sally Wilkinson, Pauline Oddy, Maureen Gainey

Dancers

Nathalie Likutu, Leanne Rowley, Beth Tweddell, Rachel Thompson (Withernsea High School)

Nicola Hoffman, Laura Hoffman, Elise Robson, Emily Downey, Leanne Cadamarteri, Heather Limbrick (Kate Hammond Academy of Dance, Nafferton)

Sofia Edstrand (Balbir Singh Dance Company)

Georgia Mason, Victoria Herridge, Philippa Lund, Hazel Mitchison, Leanne Rowley, Rebecca Jenkins

The film features: Nathalie Likutu, Beth Tweddell, Rachel Thompson, Victoria Herridge, Philippa Lund, Sofia Edstrand, Hazel Mitchison and Rebecca Jenkins.

AMY'S LAST DIVE

FROM THE BIOGRAPHY
AMY JOHNSON: QUEEN OF THE AIR
BY MIDGE GILLIES

(2003, London: Weidenfeld & Nicholson)

Characters

THE FLAMBOROUGH FISHER GIRLS DANCE TROUPE OF 1934

PAULA
a contemporary young woman from a Thames estuary town, aged 24

AMY JOHNSON

JIM MOLLISON
her husband

A GROUP OF YOUNG PEOPLE IN 2010
(from a Thames estuary town)

Prologue

Flamborough, October 18th, 1934

Light fog. A group of young women lie in a circle with their heads together; we can barely see them. A low hum gradually becomes a sustained aeroplane sound. One by one, they gradually get up, making an aeroplane noise and 'doing an Amy' with their arms outstretched. They are dressed in white trousers and blue knitted jumpers (ganseys).

WOMEN: 'Doing an Amy', 'doing an Amy', 'doing an Amy' *(repeated)*

They gradually slow down and become a standing circle. One young woman is left flying, and she keeps falling into the others in a circle, as if crashing. They play a circle game so that as one girl is about to crash into another, the girl approached becomes 'Amy' and heads off towards someone else. We hear aeroplane sound and the opening 15 seconds of the melody of 'Amy, wonderful Amy' (Jack Hylton) repeated, in a version composed for the ensemble. The following words are spoken by individual dancers.

Amy, wonderful Amy!

Who IS she?

Shop girl.

Hockey player.

Typist.

Mechanic.

Sportswoman.

Our aeroplane girl.

She's sassy.

She's beautiful.

Is she?

She's the World's Wonder-Winged Sweetheart.

Bet she doesn't have to wash the dishes!

That's 'cos she's Joan of Arc.

Joan of Arc?

The helmet... the flying helmet... armour.

Umm...

Amy Johnson wore a flying helmet and Joan of Arc wore armour... and they're both heroines.

Right...

Who do you want to be when you grow up?

I am grown up.

You know what I mean!

I want to be Amy, of course.

Well, I'd like to be Edith Cavell.

The famous nurse?

And spy.

She saved two hundred of our soldiers from the Germans.

That's why they shot her.

Well, I'd like to be Joan of Arc.

And get burnt at the stake!

But she was so devoted, and brave.

Not as brave as Amy.

Amy's the bravest girl ever.

Amy's the British Girl Lindbergh.

And she's a Hull lass.

From the Land of Green Ginger.

Her parents live in Brid!

A proper Yorkshire lass.

And a crasher.

Sometimes she only just makes it.

She's not very good at landing, is she?

Not really.

It's a wonder she's not been killed.

Oh wonderful Amy.

Wonderful Amy!

Our lone flier.

(All) Lone flier.

(Sung, with CHORUS*)*
Aeroplane dance performed by young women.

'There's a little lady who has captured every heart –
Amy Johnson, it's you.
We have watched and waited
since the day you made your start –
Amy Johnson, it's true!

Amy, wonderful Amy,
how can you blame us for loving you?
Since you've won the praise of every nation
you have filled our hearts with admiration.

Amy, wonderful Amy,
we're proud of the way you flew.
Believe us, Amy,

you cannot blame us, Amy
for falling in love with you.'

Oh Amy, wonderful Amy!

Do you remember her solo flight to Australia?

1930.

Four long years ago.

1930.

I was twelve.

And I was fourteen.

Seems like it was just yesterday, to me.

Amy and Jason, together all the way to Australia.

Jason?

Yes, Jason! Her Gypsy Moth, she called him Jason.

'Millions thrilled at her heroics!'

Do you remember?

All that posh talking in the middle of the song!

They deliberately put posh voices on.

'She's landed at Vienna.

There she is at Baghdad.

Now she's over Karachi.

She's reached Port Darwin.

Bravo!

She's up again.

She's off to Brisbane.

Here she comes, here she comes.

Something wrong.

Gracious, what's wrong?

She's crashed...

No, she's safe!'

Oh Amy, wonderful Amy!

CHORUS: *(Sung)*
'Amy, wonderful Amy,
how can you blame us for loving you?
Since you've won the praise of every nation
you have filled our hearts with admiration.'

(All) Oh if only we could be like Amy.

If only the Fisher Girls of Flame-brugh could be like Amy.

But we're just Girl Guides!

I'm proud to be a Girl Guide.

And I'm proud to be part of the Flame-brugh Fisher Girls Dance Troupe.

My family have been dancers for ever... I think.

Just think, Traves've danced every New Year's Day for years and years.

And Emmersons.

And Smiths.

And Mainprizes.

And Evere –

But we're the first women's team... ever!

'Cos Flame-brugh boys aren't interested any more.

'Cos they're not men enough to dance!

I'd never marry a lad from Flame-brugh!

Come on, we need to practise – we're going to perform at Leeds Town Hall all next week.

Bet that's grand.

And we're going to stay there.

We're going to stay in Leeds for a whole week.

We'll have bacon for breakfast... every day.

I'm going to have three slices of toast.

It's for Missions to Seamen.

It's for an exhibition.

Eeh, Flame-brugh lasses at Leeds!

Hope they like our ganseys!

We'd better get practising, then. Music please!

One of the young women distributes wooden longswords to the others. They perform the Flamborough sword dance with three stops, or 'freezes'. During each freeze, the chorus sing one of the following three verses.

CHORUS: And what would I like to be?
Soldier, sailor, vicar,
laundress, char or picker.
And what shall I be?
A woman will never be a vicar.

And what would I like to be?
Trumpeter, artist, judge,
housewife, maid or drudge.
And what shall I be?
A woman will never be a judge.

And what would I like to be?
Mechanic, pilot, cricketer,

shop girl, skivvy, knitter.
And what shall I be?
A woman will never be a cricketer.

At the end of the dance, the fog increases and AMY *almost invisibly drifts into the sword lock, or 'star'. The girls pull the swords away.* AMY *takes two of the swords and uses them as wings. The girls exit slowly, leaving* AMY *centre stage, engulfed by white light. Snow, and faint aeroplane noise. The three chorus phrases below overlap and repeat.*

CHORUS: A yellow bird/above the windy road/of the waves.

The CHORUS *quietly sing the phrase 'mesmerising whiteness' underneath the tenor.*

TENOR: A lone voyager, a lost voyager,
(Unseen) a lone voyager in mesmerising whiteness
parts the hair of the snow with her plane.

A lost voyager, a lone voyager,
a lost voyager in mesmerising whiteness
peers through ice till her eyes burn with the strain.

As winter daylight ebbs away, her fuel's almost spent.

CHORUS: Terror! Terror! Terror!

TENOR: In deepest, whitest winter
a silk flower opens,
a silk flower opens.

A suggestion of a parachutist drifting down.

(TENOR:)　　She falls, she falls, she falls
　　　　　　　into the freezing sea.

AMY:　　　　*(Getting fainter with each repeat)*

　　　　　　　Hurry, please, hurry.

　　　　　　　Hurry, please, hurry.

　　　　　　　Hurry, please, hurry.

　　　　　　　Hurry, please, hurry.

Rough sea music.

Gradual darkness. AMY *disappears slowly, still repeating her words. We hear male voices at intervals, shouting and repeating the words: 'It's a woman' and 'For God's sake lad, tell them to pull'.* AMY *hides.*

JO section

'The Ghost'

A track by a Thames estuary beach, December 21st, midwinter's eve, 2010.

JO (of JO)

Jo

The beach has an assortment of detritus on it, including half a boat with the name Seafarer *on the side, plastic, seaweed, a jam jar, rope, timber, part of the yellow wing of an aeroplane with the number 35 on it (not recognisable at this point) and part of a broken ladder.* JIM MOLLISON *is lying in the bottom of the half-boat, curled up and unseen.* PAULA *is jogging in the fog.*

PAULA: Midwinter's eve and I'm jogging!
Midwinter's eve... and it's freezing.

(Spoken) I must be mad!
(Sung) Out of/my tiny/little mind.

Running along by the edge of the sea.
Running for England (Nah!) running for me.

Running along by the edge of the sea,
running along, running along for me.

I will not spend so much time on Facebook.
I'll stop eating takeaways and learn to cook.

Working on that till is killing me
and I've had enough of this grey, grey sea.

Running along by the edge of the sea.
Running along for me, running along for me,
for me.

Two thousand and ten's been a horrible year.
I really really need to get away from here.

She stops to take a breath.

(PAULA:) Oh my muddy Thames estuary beach,
my treasure beach, my fossil beach.
Oh my bitterly cold Kent shore.
Oh my bitterly cold Kent shore.

Running along, running,
running along, running along for me.

I will not get off my face EVERY Friday night.
I'll get a boyfriend who's not a waste of space,
who's not a waste of space.

I'm gonna run a half-marathon,
though it will probably kill me.

Oh my muddy Thames estuary beach,
my treasure beach, my fossil beach.
Oh my bitterly cold Kent shore.

I will not spend so much time on Facebook.
I'll stop eating takeaways and learn to cook

I won't get off my face EVERY Friday night.
I'll get a boyfriend who's not a waste of space,
who's not a waste of space.

I will start saving up for a house,
saving for a house.

(Spoken) What? No I won't.

Oh my muddy Thames estuary beach,
my treasure beach, my fossil beach
Oh my bitterly cold Kent shore.

(PAULA:) Oh my muddy Thames estuary,
muddy Thames estuary,
muddy, bloody, muddy Thames estuary,
muddy Thames estuary beach.

Twenty four and still here. Twenty four!
Running for me, for me, for me,
Running along, for me.

Twenty four and still here!

She begins running again.

Ha

PAULA sees something off the path, at the edge of the water. This stops her running; she needs to catch her breath; she has stitch.

Kyu

It is AMY's pigskin bag. PAULA picks it up, looks at it, and – as she is about to open it – becomes aware of a presence. This frightens her and she clutches onto the bag.

Duet

AMY: I trusted myself to the air, to the air.
(Offstage,
quietly) I trusted myself to the air, to the air

for the first time, and the last time,

for the first time, and the last time.

PAULA *sniffs the bag.*

PAULA: Strange smell.

Bladderwrack... and age.

Leather... and mystery.

Strange... scent.

Vanilla... Chanel no 5?

I'll take it home. It will be my treasure...

my treasure found at the edge of the sea.

HA (of JO)

In a suggestion of her ATA flying clothes, AMY *appears, startling* PAULA. AMY's *head is bleeding.*

Jo

PAULA:
(Spoken) Whooah! Steam punk!

AMY: I ask you to leave it where you found it.

PAULA: I'm taking it home.

Ha

AMY: It belongs to me.

PAULA: How do I know it's yours?

AMY: It's all I have. My pigskin bag.

PAULA: Why do you want it?

'Cos it goes with your weird outfit?

Kyu

AMY:
(frantic) It holds my maps... my charts,

(melancholic) my maps... my charts,

my maps, my charts.

There is no flying without the pigskin bag,

no return to the sky,

the sky, the sky, the sky.

Please give it back to me.

KYU (of JO)

Jo

AMY *shivers uncontrollably.* PAULA *goes to comfort her but* AMY *gestures for her to keep away.*

Ha

Duet

PAULA: You think you've dropped out of the sky?

Are you wired, girl? Are you high?

Is it ket or poppers, crack or smack?

What is the monkey on your back?

AMY: I am a pilot without her plane,

a bird without wings.

How shall I climb the air

without my pigskin bag?

How shall I climb the air?

AMY *and* PAULA's *lines overlap and are repeated.*

Pause

PAULA: You're bleeding

PAULA *goes to help her but* AMY *gestures for her to keep away again.*

Kyu

PAULA: You need a bandage.

AMY *gestures towards the bag.* PAULA *opens it.* AMY *gestures again.* PAULA *takes a smart white scarf out of the bag. She lays it over the nearest edge of the boat.* AMY *snatches it and holds it in her hand.*

AMY: How shall I climb the air?

PAULA: Don't you know people can't fly!

Look... I live nearby.

I'll get you a hot drink

and a warm blanket.

And when I come back,

if you're still by this track

and haven't flown up to the stars

you can tell me who you are,

you can tell me, tell me,

tell me who you are

and I'll give you your bag.

Pause.

What got you into this state?

Was it a man? It's usually a man.

Pause.

(Spoken) I won't be long, twenty minutes...

PAULA *leaves.*

AMY: My maps... my charts...
(Sadly)

How shall I climb the air

without my pigskin bag?

Pause.

Was it a man? A man?

Oh there were many men.

And there was one man –

my devilish husband.

A man with a bandage.

A man with a bandage!

She drops the scarf into the boat.

HA section

'Dual Control'

JO (of HA)

AMY *sits up in the boat, as if in bed.*

Jo

AMY: 'Tell me who you are.' 'Tell me who you are.' Who am I?

(AMY:) *Pause*

I am the horse-faced hag, apparently.
(shouted into the boat)

That's what my ex-husband called me: 'the horse-faced hag'.

You should have seen us both in bed, after the crash

when we almost reached New York

at the end of our dual Atlantic flight, east to west.

He looked like a... like an Egyptian mummy.

Muffled groans and cries from the boat. JIM *rises slowly up like 'the mummy', with his head almost completely bandaged.*

He looked like Tutankhamen.

You look like King Tut, Jim!

He continues to moan. AMY *laughs. She puts a stalk in a jam jar and places it on the side of the boat. She looks at herself in a scrap of mirror.*

And look at me, windblown hair, dirty nails.

No, no, no!

She takes out some lipstick from a pocket and puts it on.

(AMY:)　　　What we want is a manicured, powdered, perfect girl.

She puts her nail varnish on.

You can take the photos now.

Camera flashes.

Oh the white roses are from the Roosevelts.

More camera flashes as they freeze in a pose.

Pause

He's best like that, jaw wired.

And to think I wanted a man of the world

who'd make my toes curl!

Ha

Oh but there was a time
before that blur of light
at the end of our Atlantic flight,
before that terrible night
when we landed in the swamp
(Shouts)　　which he was entirely responsible for.

Oh there was a time,
before they found us in a ditch,
there was a time
when we were the Flying Scot
and the Lone Flyer,

(AMY:) the Flying Sweethearts,
Brandy Mollison
and the British Girl Lindbergh.

Oh yes there was a time,
there was a time
before they found us in that ditch
where I cradled his body in my lap –
'Hurry, please hurry'
'Hurry, please hurry' –
I thought he was going to die.

(*Shouts*) I thought you were going to die,
you two-timing half-cut dinner-suited
suede-shoed cad!

Oh Jim, oh Jim.

She slowly and lovingly takes his bandages off.

I thought you were my Valentino

when we lunched at Quagalinos.

I was the girl on your arm.

How I fell for your charm!

You called me Johnnie.

Johnnie for Johnson.

Johnnie, Johnnie.

Kyu

AMY & JIM: *Duet*

AMY: Oh Jim.

JIM: Oh Johnnie.

AMY: Oh Jim, oh Jim.

JIM: Oh Johnnie, Johnnie, Johnnie.

AMY: We have dual controls.

JIM: Such dual controls.

BOTH: We are a single-engine biplane

with a Gipsy Major Engine.

AMY: We have dual controls.

JIM: Oh such dual controls.

I love your steel bracing.

AMY: I love your engine cowling.

JIM: I love your cockpit docking.

AMY: I love our interlocking.

JIM: I love our interlocking.

Dual controls!

AMY: Such dual controls!

(AMY:)	Oh the sweep back and stagger of your wings.
JIM:	Oh oh, your shock-absorbing springs.
	Oh oh, we have such dual controls.
AMY:	Yes yes, such dual controls.
	Oh Jim, oh Jim.
JIM:	Oh Johnnie, Johnnie, Johnnie.
	Let me feel your struts.
AMY:	Ow! Oh oh, your swaged rod.
JIM:	Let me feed your carburettor.
AMY:	Yes yes yes, you are my tiger.
JIM:	You are my moth.
AMY: *(Growls)*	Dual controls!
JIM:	Such such dual controls!
AMY:	Oh Jim, oh Jim, oh Jim.
JIM:	Oh Johnnie, Johnnie, Johnnie.
AMY:	Oh oh oh oh your parallel foot action.
JIM:	Aah aaah aaah your longitudinal trim.

AMY:	Ow! Oh oh oh oh ooooooh!
JIM:	Aaaaaaaaaaah! Aaah!
	Tiptop!
AMY:	You are my tiger.
JIM:	You are my moth.
AMY:	You are my king.
JIM:	You are my queen.
BOTH:	We are the king and queen of the air.
AMY:	The king and queen of the air. Oh Jim.
JIM:	Oh Johnnie, Johnnie, Johnnie.
AMY: *(Angrily)*	Oh Jim!
	Why did I marry you?
JIM:	Because I asked you. Because I asked you.
AMY:	Because... you were Drake and Raleigh, Scott and Shackleton.
JIM:	Because you were the Lone Girl Flyer and I was the Flying Scot.
AMY:	You were a drunk, an unfaithful, arrogant, selfish, dangerous...

(AMY:) lollygagger!

You were Brandy Mollison, the pilot with a flask in his hand.

You were a record-breaker.

You were my heartbreaker.

HA (of HA)

Jo

JIM is drinking from a flask.

JIM: All seemed so bally straightforward:

set off from Wales in a westerly direction,

stop off in New York, New York, New York,

then circle the globe,

just you and me, circle the globe,

just you and me, just you and me,

Jim and Johnnie, Johnnie and Jim.

AMY: What balderdash was that you said that I believed?

JIM: 'I suppose the essential spirit of such a flight must be faith – faith

(JIM:) in oneself, one's companion, in the aeroplane and in the engine.'

AMY: One's companion – tick
The aeroplane – tick
The engine – tick

'Oneself.'

Well there's the problem, there's the rub, Jim!

Self, self, self!   Me, me, me!

She knocks the flowers over and takes the sheet of plastic off both of them.

Ha

(The flight has something of the aspects of a clown routine and the music should reflect this.)

JIM *stands by the side of the boat, and tests the breeze with a white handkerchief.*

JIM: Still as a graveyard. About bally time!

Thought we'd never get off the ground.

Well, Johnnie. New York, here we come.

She hands him his flying helmet (it is a found object).

AMY: Put that flask away, Jim.

JIM: Just a tot, to toast our coming success!

(JIM:) Just a tot, just a tot.

AMY puts her flying helmet on (it is also a found object). JIM sits in front of her in the boat.

> Just you and me and mighty wilderness now, Johnnie.
>
> You and me and the sky and the sea.
>
> Let's get this bird up in the air!

Take-off music. AMY and JIM mime piloting the plane up into the air and speak the following 'Goodbye words'. AMY waves to the crowds. JIM drinks as he is flying with one hand.

AMY: Goodbye to Wales.

JIM: Goodbye to playing golf.

AMY: Goodbye to the photographers.

JIM: Goodbye to the reporters.

AMY: Goodbye to all those speeches.

JIM: Goodbye to the crowd!

AMY: Goodbye to the funfair!

JIM: Goodbye to the beach.

>   Goodbye to the donkey rides.

AMY:	Oh how I hate flying over water,
(Sung)	
	how I hate flying over water.

Kyu

JIM:	Just you and me and the sky and the sea
	Just you and me and the sky and the sea,
	and the sky and the sea, Johnnie, Johnnie.

AMY begins to fall asleep and jerks awake.

| AMY: | And utter boredom! |

JIM takes another drink from his flask. The 'plane' is suddenly buffeted by headwinds.

JIM:	We're somewhere in the middle of the big pond.
	New York that way... I think.
AMY:	All those hungry waves below, like vultures.
JIM:	Time to swap over.

They bump into each other.

| | And again! |

They repeat the same routine.

| AMY: | Time for some face powder. |

JIM: Time for some coffee.

And down through the clouds at last.

AMY is looking through a hole in the bottom of the 'plane'. She scribbles on a piece of paper and hands it to JIM.

Icebergs!

AMY: It's like a huge bath strewn with snowflakes.

JIM: Land!

They shake hands solemnly.

KYU (of HA)

Jo

JIM: We're over the good ol' US of A.

We'll soon be hoofin' it in the Big Apple, kitten.

AMY: We won't make it, you half-portion!

There's not enough juice.

We're going to run out of juice!

JIM: Piffle!

AMY: The headwinds forced us to use too much.

We should refuel while it's still light.

(AMY:)	*Pause*
	Jim, we've been in the air for thirty-eight hours.
	We need to refuel! Refuel!
JIM:	Press on woman, press on!
	Just forty miles to New York, New York.

Sudden sputtering noises.

AMY:	Ease the nose higher.
	Higher!
	We won't make it. We won't make it!
JIM:	We'll have to land at Bridgeport. Good ol' Connecticut.
	Pause.
	I can't bally see where the airfield begins and the swamp ends.
(Shouted)	I can't bally see Johnnie.

Ha

Flashing lights, aeroplane noise. The 'plane' rocks wildly.

AMY:	Circle again.

JIM: I'm circling.

AMY: What?

JIM: I am circling, you horse-faced hag.

AMY: What did you just call me?

JIM: Brace yourself Johnnie. Brace yourself.

Groaning plane noises: momentary darkness, unbearable brightness and then a sickening crunch, followed by pitch darkness.

Kyu

AMY *whimpers. Torch lights.* AMY *cradles* JIM's *body in her lap.*

AMY: Hurry, please, we're over here...

Hurry, please hurry.

...my God, hurry please.

(Screams) He's dying!

Kyu (coda)

AMY *and* JIM *are sitting up in 'bed' as at the beginning of the* **HA** *section, but with* JIM *only partly bandaged.*

JIM: We nearly made New York.

We almost made New York.

AMY: You nearly killed yourself.

You almost killed both of us.

Pause.

Crawl away. I said crawl away.

He does so.

AMY: I'm flying solo again Jim, solo forever,

solo forever, solo forever.

JIM: *(Overlapping with Amy, as she repeats 'I'm flying solo...')*

But we had such dual controls,

such dual controls.

AMY: Oh Jim, oh Jim.

She cries as the lights fade.

Interlude

The same Thames estuary beach, midwinter's eve, 2010.

Music with a strong, pulsing beat.

A group of YOUNG PEOPLE *arrive noisily, using their mobiles, listening to their iPods, singing, dancing, trying* on each other's clothes and fooling around. Names can be added to the following lines.

LEADER: It's the solstice, the winter solstice. We gotta make a bonfire.

What?

LEADER: It's a ritual... magic, druids and things.

Why?

LEADER: To keep the sun going 'cos it's so dark it might not come back.

That's stupid.

I'll google it. Winter... solstice. Come on... come on.

'The winter solstice occurs exactly when the axial tilt of a planet's polar hemisphere is farthest away from the star that it orbits. Earth's maximum axial tilt to our star, the Sun, during a solstice is 23° 26'.'

Yeah, it's when the sun is lowest in the sky. Anyone knows that.

LEADER: Let's do the ritual then.

Whatever.

They build the bonfire.

To me, to me.

God, there's some rank stuff here.

What's this?

Looks like... part of a really old... plane wing?

This old boat's so heavy.

It's rotten... and it stinks.

Ow, I've cut myself.

Never thought I'd be doing litter-picking tonight.

Rhythmic music and fire song.

They build the fire. The YOUNG PEOPLE *have the following words which are chanted, and the* CHORUS *sing the descriptive phrases repeatedly. The* CHORUS *continues quietly under the ritual, like a drone.*

YOUNG PEOPLE	CHORUS
We're buildin' a fire,	Midwinter fire
our midwinter fire, our seashore pyre,	Seashore pyre
higher an' higher, higher an' higher.	Midwinter fire
We're stackin' our fire,	Burning tower
our burnin' tower, our sky-lickin' fire,	Sky-licking fire

higher an' higher, higher an' higher.	Midwinter fire
We're buildin' a fire,	Toe-toasting fire
our sky-lickin', toe-toastin', midwinter fire,	Midwinter fire
to fire up the sun that's losin' its fire,	Fire up the sun
to fire up the sun that's losin' its fire,	that's losing its fire.

LEADER: Now we gotta do the ritual. You hold a piece of wood above your head and say your worst nightmare out loud, and then you throw the wood on the fire.

Burn all the bad stuff.

Yeah, burn all the bad stuff.

This is really stupid!

Just do it.

LEADER: Like this.

My worst nightmare is – *(she states her nightmare)*

Wood into fire, I'll burn my nightmare.

Each participant says their own nightmare, using the same form of words and throwing a piece of wood onto the fire:

LEADER: And then you get a stone and you hold it in your hand and you say your dream out loud and then you place your stone carefully on the fire, and the fire 'll heat it up.

What sort of dream?

LEADER: What you wish for, your... highest ambition.

So the bonfire cooks your dream.

Yeah, bake our dreams.

This is soooo mad!

Let's just do it.

LEADER: Like this.

My dream is to – *(she states her dream)*

Stone into fire, I'll heat my dream.

Each participant says their own dream, using the same form of words and placing a stone on the fire.

Awesome!

Like that's gonna work!

It might.

The chorus stop singing.

LEADER: We gotta trust the ritual.

The fog's coming down. Let's go and get some voddies.

Yeah, supplies.

Watch a couple o' films and then come back.

What time's the solstice?

LEADER: 5.30 am, so we should be back here for 5 I reckon.

You must be jokin' me. We'll come back at midnight, end of.

Yeah. Come back at midnight and burn all the bad stuff.

Light up the sky.

Yeah, light up the sky.

Burn our nightmares.

And bake our stones... I mean dreams!

Boom! Boom!

See youse all laters.

Laters!

The fog becomes thicker again. The young people leave slowly.

KYU section

'Lone flier' or 'True desire'

JO (of KYU)

Jo

Fog. PAULA *returns with the blanket and flask to find no one there. Puzzled, she looks at the bonfire and the stones placed on it.*

PAULA: Hello. Hello!

                  Sorry I took so long.

                  My so-called boyfriend was at the house.

                  I think he came round to borrow money.

                  I'm thinking of going away… leaving here.

                  I want to get that feeling… like when I'm running…

                  I want that feeling all the time.

                  Hello?

She searches. A low aeroplane hum begins.

Ha

The sound rises, and includes other sounds that suggest

different continents. AMY *emerges from the bonfire and stands on top of it, like Joan of Arc, backed by the stake of an aeroplane wing.* PAULA *screams.*

AMY: Give me my pigskin bag.

PAULA: Who are you?

Kyu

AMY: My name is Amy.

Pause.

The Lone Flyer.

The Queen of the Air.

Pause.

PAULA: You can't be. You died...

somewhere out there... in the estuary.

Years and years ago... in the war.

They never found your body.

We did you at junior school.

You were the bravest girl ever.

I drew your plane... you called it... Jason.

Jason.

AMY: I must have my maps.

Paula gives her the bag, and then runs back. Amy takes her maps out and places one near to her. She stretches her arms out.

HA (of KYU)

Jo

AMY: The real love of my life was always Jason,

my thin, precious wooden crate,

my second skin, my faithful mate,

my bottle-green Gypsy Moth,

my plane with wings of silver-grey,

strong wings of silver-grey.

She raises her arms up.

Oh my thin, precious wooden crate,

my second skin, my faithful mate.

Oh Jason, Jason,

let's fly all the way to Australia,

just you and me, Amy and Jason,

like in the good old bad old days,

(AMY:) the good old bad old days.

Ha

She brings her arms down and takes her hands to the sides of her head.

> Now I am a speck
>
> and when I am a speck
>
> I am most myself.
>
> I am a speck
>
> and when I am a speck
>
> I am most myself.

She raises her arms up.

> Follow the railway line to Syria
>
> and over the Taurus mountains
>
> to the unsurveyed desert.

She throws a map away.

> Let's make for sun-scorched Basra.

PAULA: Basra. Basra!

That's what messed with the boyfriend's head.

The following lines overlap with AMY's *lines.*

(PAULA:)　　They should never of sent him.

　　　　　　They should never of sent him.

　　　　　　Sunny I-raq, Sunny I-raq

　　　　　　scrambled his brain!

　　　　　　They should never of sent him.

AMY:　　　We're on our way to the Gardens of Babylon.

　　　　　　We're on our way to the Garden of Eden.

　　　　　　We're on our way to the Garden of Eden.

　　　　　　We're on our way to the Gardens of Babylon.

Kyu

PAULA:　　Why? Why do you fly?

AMY:　　　Because a little girl read *The Tales of the Arabian Nights*.

　　　　　　Because the temples of Bangkok look like Christmas trees.

　　　　　　Because...

　　　　　　because the greatest gamble of all is the gamble of life,

　　　　　　the greatest gamble of all is the gamble of life.

(AMY:) Because...

because I possess endurance, patience and resource,

endurance, patience and resource.

Pause.

Because when I am a speck I am most myself.

KYU (of KYU)

Jo

PAULA: But aren't you terrified?

AMY: I'm very afraid of the sea.

The sea's greedy for me, greedy for me.

We're still on our way to Australia, Jason and me,

just Jason and me, when we disappear over the Java sea.

Lost and alone above the violent ocean,

I drift, I dream, I circle round and round, round and round the black, angry waves.

Typhoons, hurricanoes, water-spouts.

Get back you hurricanoes!

(AMY:) Polly put the kettle on,
Polly put the kettle on –

Little Bo-Peep has lost her sheep
And can't tell where to –

Tyger! Tyger! burning bright
In the forests of the night,
What immortal hand or eye
could frame thy fearful symmetry?
In what distant deeps or skies –

Half a league, half a league,
Half a league onward,
All in the valley of Death, of Death, of Death –

I drift, I dream, I circle round and round, round and round,

lost and alone above the violent ocean.

And then I see a perfect rainbow,

a perfect rainbow.

She drops her arms to her sides.

While I was over the Java Sea,

a woman had a vision of me.

She saw me in a cloud of light

and knew everything would be alright.

(PAULA:)　　Your maps...

She takes a map out and looks at it.

Sumatra, Java, Semarang... Surabaya.

Don't be afraid to fail.

Endurance, patience, resource.

Half-marathon. Soooo easy!

Watch out, world!

Paula is on fire,

Paula is on fire!

She jogs off.

(AMY): Jason. Jason? Jason. Jason?

She raises her arms.

Kyu

Take me back into the whirling snow.

Endurance, patience, resource.

Don't be afraid to fail.

Endurance, patience, resource.

Take me back into the whirling snow.

AMY *disappears into the fog. The following words overlap and interweave, with* AMY *finishing first.*

TENOR: *(Unseen)*	A lone voyager, a lost voyager, a lone voyager in mesmerising whiteness parts the hair of the snow with her plane.
AMY: *(Unseen)*	Don't be afraid to fail. Endurance, patience, resource.
CHORUS:	A yellow bird/above the windy road/of the waves.

Coda

PAULA: Amy... Amy?

You left your bag.

(AMY:)   They said I was like Joan of Arc,

   Joan of Arc.

A suggestion of flames, stillness.

Ha

PAULA: You were a celebrity.

A rising sound suggesting applause, cheers and shouting.

AMY: Australia! Australia! Australia!

   Now everyone wants a piece of me,

   everyone wants a piece of me.

   Australia! Australia! Australia!

   Now everyone wants a piece of me,

   everyone wants a piece of me.

   They gawp and claw, gawp and claw.

   I stare out of every shop window and…

   I feel I am not myself, I feel I am not myself.

   Pause.

   I must fly. I must fly. I must fly.

   I must fly. I must fly. I must fly.